What Others Are S

"If you want to achieve happiness and live a life of integrity, read this book. Whether you are a business owner, executive, or a college student, this book will act as your guiding companion to help you live the life of your dreams!"

     – **Shannon S. Carlson, author of** *Living Your Life in Balance*

"Dennis Kelley hits the nail on the head! A powerful, brilliant book that walks you through the steps to attaining success and ultimate happiness in every area of your life. He shows you how to do it on your own terms and provides the keys to simplifying your life and business. A must read for every entrepreneur and business professional who seeks clarity and unlimited success."

   – **Deborah Reynolds, International Image Consultant, author of** *Getting Noticed, Known and Remembered; How to Build Your Business Image from the Inside Out*

"With this book as your personal success compass, you will become unstoppable and soar in life! I recommend this book for anyone interested in achieving true success in business and life."

     – **Patrick Snow, best-selling author of** *Creating Your Own Destiny*

"Dennis Kelley offers substance and not fluff in this well-paced, must read book written for anyone who has ever dreamed of achieving their definition of success."

     – **Michael Schindler, author of** *Operation Military Family*

"Dennis Kelley's brilliant book reminds us of the importance of creating our own reality. It's NEVER too late to begin."

     – **Joan Bunney, author of** *SEXY In Your Sixties*

"This book speaks to the heart of what Dennis is – a teacher who is learning about himself as well as others and sees opportunities in every challenge. I recommend this book for any business owner or professional looking to make positive changes in their life to achieve success."

     – **Donna Frankoski**

"Dennis is a proven leader who has shared his insights for professional and personal excellence in this exciting book. It is a 'must read' for anyone who has ever tackled the dilemma of how to combine high levels of achievement with extraordinary personal life satisfaction."

     – **Lauren H. Jackson, Ph.D.**

"Dennis has taught me to challenge myself and to push to another level to achieve a higher level of success, rather than take success at face value. One of the most important things I have learned from Dennis is the sky is the limit and that I control how far I can go!"

– **Kristi Bifolchi**

"Dennis was a great mentor and powerful coach to me. Through regular one-on-one coaching sessions, and his thoughtful advice and encouragement, I was inspired to push myself toward continued success and growth in my career. I am pleased that Dennis has now recorded, in this book, his philosophy about the nature of success and how to achieve that success. Dennis certainly helped me build the foundation for my success and showed me how to focus on my continued growth over the last twenty years."

– **Marya Young, Executive Vice President, Shore Morgan Young – Innovative Wealth Solutions**

"I had the privilege of working with Dennis for several years. I used to be scared to death of public speaking, which was beginning to affect my career advancement opportunities. When I shared this with Dennis – a life-changing event took place. Dennis immediately coached me and provided me with consistent opportunities to practice this new skill. In a few short months of coaching from Dennis, I was able to overcome my fears and get out of my own way in terms of career advancement opportunities. Today, I speak in front of large groups frequently and with ease thanks to Dennis!"

– **Stacy Radabaugh, SVP Sales Manager, Charter One Bank**

"When Dennis first hired me and began working with me, he not only became the best boss I ever had, but also a mentor and a friend. Much of the success I have in my career today, I thank Dennis for."

– **Jeff Swindell**

"Dennis has packed a hefty amount of common sense and straight talk into *Achieving Unlimited Success*. I found innumerable gems and sudden insights scattered throughout. For example, Dennis said, 'As we grow older, we begin to doubt ourselves and let fear of failure or embarrassment slow us down.' Wow! I am 61 years old, have come out of retirement to start another career in a field completely new to me, and that new awareness will be worth money to me. If you will get the book and read the book, I bet you will profit from the book."

– **Don Burrows, author of *Plan While You Still Can* – *16 End-of-Life Checklists You Need Now***

A Practical Approach for Entrepreneurs and
Business Professionals of All Levels

ACHIEVING
UNLIMITED
SUCCESS

How to Get Out of Your
Own Way and Live the Life
of Your Dreams

DENNIS A. KELLEY

AVIVA
PUBLISHING
New York

Achieving Unlimited Success
How to Get Out of Your Own Way and Live the Life of Your Dreams

This book is available for quantity discounts, for bulk purchases and for branding by businesses and organizations. For further information, or to learn more about *Achieving Unlimited Success* and *The D. Kelley Group* contact:

The D. Kelley Group
Dennis A. Kelley
1206 N. Main Street, Suite 123
North Canton, OH 44720
Telephone toll free: (866) 554-1995
www.AchievingUnlimitedSuccess.com

ISBN: 978-1-890427-80-1

Library of Congress # 2007942667

Editor: Shannon Evans
Cover Design: Dunn-Design Associates
Typesetting: Ad Graphics, Inc.

Every attempt has been made to properly source all quotes.

Printed in the United States of America

First Edition

Dedication

I would like to dedicate this book to my family:

To my wonderful wife, Nancy: Thank you for being so supportive of me and the pursuit of my dreams! You have been my inspiration and I appreciate your love and support. Your love is my strength.

To my children, Christina, Jennifer and Andrew: You are so important to me and are a major reason why I have worked so hard to achieve success. I hope you find benefit in the message of this book and find the true happiness and success of your dreams!

To my parents, Robert and Georgia Kelley: Thank you for all your love and support. You have been a positive inspiration to me all my life.

Acknowledgements
And Many Thanks…

I would like to thank and recognize all of the following people for their support, encouragement, and belief in my dreams. I would also like to thank everyone listed here who has helped me with the completion of this book and in my career:

Patrick Snow; for your coaching, guidance and encouragement in putting this whole project together. You are awesome!

Shannon Evans; thank you for your patience and direction in fine-tuning this manuscript and helping bring the project to completion.

Hobie and Kathi Dunn, Cindy Johnson, Graham VanDixhorn, Tony Wall, and Jim and Barb Weems; for all your input and guidance on putting the project together and bringing all the elements to life. This project would not have been completed without your support.

To all my past mentors including, Henry Steeler, Alex Zardinskas, Gary Vaccaro, Steve Nesbitt, Kathy Lundberg and many others who have helped me in my career and life.

Dawn Heartwell; my business coach and friend who has pushed me, mentored me and challenged me to always take action on my dreams.

To my family, friends, clients and trusted advisors; you have all been an inspiration to me and I thank you for your support.

Table of Contents

Introduction

"The starting point of great success and achievement has always been the same. It is for you to dream big dreams. There is nothing more important and nothing that works faster than for you to cast off your own limitations, than for you to begin dreaming and fantasizing about the wonderful things that you can become, have and do."

– Brian Tracy

What are the dreams you have for your life? Are you relying on fate or chance to create the life you want and to accomplish those dreams? If so, then now is the time to change your thinking and take control. Success does not just happen by chance or by fate. Success is the pursuit of a passion and a dream that requires you to take action to get the life you desire.

How many times have you said to yourself, "There's got to be something more?" Now is the time to decide what you want from life and what you need to do to make it a reality. You need to take action, but first, you need to understand what you want and how to get it. You also need to determine what is holding you back and how to remove those barriers from your path. You can then take control of your life and make it whatever you want it to be.

It amazes me when I ask someone what they want from their business or their life and they respond by saying they would be happy just making enough money to pay the bills and get a chance to take an occasional vacation. Wow … I absolutely believe there has to be more to life than that.

Everyone has the ability to make his or her own path in life. Pursuing life's passion and success should not be the destiny of a select few. When you take the appropriate steps to identify what success means to you and eliminate your self-limiting beliefs, you will be amazed at what you can achieve.

In this book, I will deal with the steps you need to take to identify your ideal life, establish your vision of success and then help you understand what self-limiting beliefs will get in your way. You will then eliminate these negative beliefs and take action to reach success. Success will be a journey and not a destination. As you grow and your world changes, so will your vision and goals. The more success you achieve, the more confidence you will have and the faster you will take action to be the best you that you can be.

Success is not just about wealth and power but also involves your interests, passions, and relationships. You deserve to have what you want from life and nothing should get in your way. There are countless examples of ordinary people – business owners, professionals, homemakers – taking control of their life and achieving astonishing success. Some of the most successful people in the world started out with virtually nothing and – through passion, commitment and positive action – reached the success they desired.

But, success needs to be very individually defined. What success means to one person isn't what it means to the next person. This book is designed to help you achieve unlimited success according to how you define it.

> *"There is only one success – to be able to*
> *spend your life in your own way."*
> **– Christopher Morley**

Once you have defined success, then you need to identify your self-limiting beliefs and build a plan to eliminate them from your thinking. Before you can start living the life of your dreams, you need to get your self-limiting beliefs out of your way so they won't hold you back.

Changing your thinking is critical to the process of achieving unlimited success. Understand though, that it's not enough to just dream about or think about what you want. You have to believe with all your heart that success is possible and you will achieve it. Once you have truly internalized this belief, you must then take action every day. Because you are now thinking positively and truly believing success will be yours, your actions will be much more powerful and you will find doors opening for you.

This book is your guide to eliminating the negative thinking patterns and taking positive action that will lead you to the life of your dreams. You will develop a practical success plan to guide you and keep you on track. Achieving unlimited success is not only possible, it is within your grasp.

Good luck on your journey, have fun and let's get started.

CHAPTER 1

Defining Success on Your Own Terms

"We all have the extraordinary coded within us ... waiting to be released."

— Jean Houston

Have you ever taken the time to stop and think about what you want from life? I mean really think about what your ideal life would be? Stop for a minute and pretend that you are celebrating your 100th birthday today. You are thinking back on your life and all that you have accomplished. Think about your relationships, your career, how you spent your time and what your legacy is going to be. What does that vision look like? What do you want it to be? Is the path you are on today leading you to achieve all that you just thought about? What will it take for you to get everything you want, and are you willing to do what it takes to get it?

In my more than 30 years in business, I have encountered many people that have achieved amazing levels of success in both business and their personal life. I always marvel at these people and all that they have accomplished. Do they have special powers? Maybe they were born with a success gene, or maybe they just happened to be in the right place at the right time and life rewarded them. Whatever it is they have, they managed to grab the golden goose and take it to the bank.

I have also met many people who had an excellent opportunity to achieve high levels of success and did not do it. Instead, they chose to take a different path and allowed real success to pass them by. What was it that caused them to avoid the success they were seeking? Was it bad timing? Were they not born with the drive needed to get what they wanted?

Self-limiting Beliefs

One thing we all have in common is that all of us have self-limiting beliefs that affect our success. No matter how successful you are, you will still have self-limiting beliefs.

Self-limiting beliefs are the thoughts that define how we feel about our worth, including our value to ourselves, our relationships, our community, and our value in the workplace. If you believe you are only worth a salary of $50,000, that becomes your limiting belief. Even if you decide you should earn $500,000, you are defining a different limiting belief level, but it is still limited.

Maybe you believe that you could never own a business, or you might believe it is not possible for you to become a millionaire. These are self-limiting beliefs. Wherever you cap your expectation, that is where you see yourself stopping and you end up putting up a mental block to achieve any more than that.

Sheldon Koggs said it well,

> *"All of the significant battles are waged within the self."*

People at all levels of income, education and background have common characteristics that distinguish those that achieved success and those that missed the mark.

In this book, we will examine the common traits of successful people and how you, too, can achieve the highest levels of success AS YOU DEFINE IT!

YOU need to define what success means to you. If you do not know what success looks like or feels like, then how will you know when you experience it? It is important to understand you control what goals you are aiming to achieve.

It is also necessary to understand that success does not just happen; it is orchestrated like a fine symphony.

> *"High Expectations Are the Key to Everything."*
> – Sam Walton

What Does Success Look Like?

To achieve success in life, you first must know what success is. What does success mean to you? What does it look like in your mind? Everyone must define success in his or her own terms.

Marketing messages bombard us daily trying to define success. Our popular culture works hard to sell a commercial version of "success."

The images seen every day in the media tell you what you should own if you are truly successful. Clothing companies tell you what you should wear and how you should look. Images and messages of "successful" people and the size and style of home they live in, how big the swimming pool is and all the associated luxuries bombard us constantly.

What is your vision of success? Is it driven by images of movie stars or business tycoons? Maybe you equate success with images of sports figures. Ask people from all around the world about popular movie stars and professional athletes and you will get an immediate and enthusiastic response.

The reason movie stars and professional athletes are successful has very little to do with what they own, where they live or how much television or media coverage they get. They are successful because they decided what they wanted and went out and got it. These people thrive on their definition of success and are passionate about it.

Michael Jordan, considered the most admired sports figure in the world, achieved the highest level of success by knowing what he wanted and pursuing it with passion. However, his success did not come without a lot of hard work and effort.

Jordan was cut from the varsity team as a sophomore at his high school. "Whenever I was working out and got tired and figured I ought to stop, I'd close my eyes and see that list in the locker room without my name on it and that usually got me going again." He eventually made the team and led it to the state championship. Jordan knew what he wanted and made it his mission to accomplish it. By staying focused on his goal, he ended up leading the Chicago Bulls to six NBA Championship titles.

The common denominator of all successful people is their passion for their dream. They have defined what they want from life and are willing to do what it takes to reach their dreams. Define what you want from your life and be willing to pursue it with the same passion and commitment.

> *"A successful life is one that is lived through understanding and pursuing one's path, not chasing after the dreams of others."*
> **– Chin-Nihn Chu**

> **You could choose to be like Lily Tomlin,
> "I've always wanted to be somebody, but I see
> now I should have been more specific."**

A life without vision is a life left to drift and take whatever is thrown your way. If you wait too long to decide what you want from life, you may look back and agree with Ms. Tomlin!

Thinking About Success on Bigger Terms

When people are asked, "What is success?" all kinds of answers result. Most people start out talking about what type of job or position they have, how much money they make, or what possessions they own. All are very valid measurements of success.

Think about success in bigger terms. What do you *truly* want from life? Success should be defined by who we are and what we believe in; that can mean many different things to different people. For some it is money, for others relationships and for others it is family or community. Still others strive for power or publicity. Many people define success through their business, career or job.

In Stephen Covey's book, *The 7 Habits of Highly Effective People*, he lists one of his seven habits as the Principal of Personal Leadership. In this principle, Covey tells us to "begin with the end in mind." This principle applies to defining success. Understand what success means to you before you begin on your success journey. By beginning with the end in mind you will be clear on what you are aiming to reach.

Webster's dictionary defines success as, "a: degree or measure of succeeding b: favorable or desired outcome; also: the attainment of wealth, favor, or eminence." This is a textbook definition, but it does lead us to a few key points.

First, success is a measure of something. In order to determine if you succeeded, you need to be able to measure progress toward a desired outcome. In order to have a desired outcome, you first need to know what outcome you actually want! You cannot succeed if you do not know what you are looking to accomplish in the first place. Webster's definition refers to, "the attainment of wealth, favor or eminence." So, what level of wealth are you aiming for? What level of favor do you want from your relationships, your community and your spiritual self? Is eminence or power and celebrity status important to you?

A successful life is one where you can be actively engaged in creative activities that contribute to the achievement of your desired outcome. According to Henry David Thoreau, "In the long run, men hit only what they aim at." Determining what it is that you are aiming for is the first step in your journey.

My Definition of Success

My wife and I have talked many times about what success means and exactly what we want to accomplish in our life together. Each of us has our own goals we want to accomplish for ourself, but we also have goals that we want to accomplish as a couple. For us, we have defined a series of objectives tied to the creation of wealth and happiness in several forms.

Relationships and Family – a part of our definition of success is a loving, happy and healthy family life. Success means making sure that our kids all receive a college degree from a high quality four-year college. Should our children choose to marry, we will provide a wedding. It means having a close family that supports and nurtures each other and a home where our children, friends, and family enjoy coming and spending time.

Wealth – we will consider ourselves wealthy when we no longer have to work to pay our bills and support our life but can quit working any time we want and not have to worry about money. For us wealth is not about how many zero's we have on our net worth. It is more a factor of providing financial security and the quality of life we desire. I do have a dollar amount in my mind I believe it will take to achieve this goal; however, it is not about accumulating huge sums of money but about supporting our life. We have been fortunate to make significant strides towards this goal and will keep a laser focus on achieving it. We should always work at something, but we should not have to work in order to survive. Wealth means working because we love what we do.

Power or Celebrity – the attainment of power or celebrity status is not a measure of success for us. However, I have a big measure of my personal success that centers around my career. I own a business coaching company and define success as helping as many business owners/executives improve the quality of their business and life as I possibly can. Seeing the owner or executive achieve goals they thought they were never going to achieve is very rewarding. It is gratifying to help them get their business or career to the next defined level of success.

Writing this book and having it published is another element of how I have defined success for myself. This book is about trying to extend the reach of my coaching business to help as many people as possible achieve their dreams of success. I can reach more people through my book than I can in person.

Another component in my career is my public speaking business. It allows me to reach large groups of people, to share my business coaching knowledge, and share my experience about how to achieve the success in business and life that everyone desires.

Community – we have defined success in this area by giving back to our community with our time and through a charitable foundation. We both volunteer at various community activities and enjoy doing so. We plan to establish a charitable foundation that will give back to our community. This will provide an opportunity to teach our children the importance of helping others as well as a greater appreciation for their community.

Define your own ideas of what success is. By spending some time thinking about and articulating your measures of success, you will become very clear on what you want *your* life to be.

Define Success First Then Figure Out How to Get There

There are no clearly defined action steps or quantitative goals as a part of this exercise. Instead, focus on the bigger picture of your life including your aspirations and dreams. When you think about your job or career, it is not important to define the specifics of the position you want but instead define what you want from a job or career. What type of work do you want to be doing? What level is it and will you own the business or work for someone else? The same thing applies to wealth creation and the other aspects of success that you desire. For now, it is important to understand what drives you and what makes you feel fulfilled. Later, we will work on drilling down to the specifics and focus on exactly what you want.

If wealth is one of your success measures, then it is important for you to realize that wealth can only come after you achieve success. Most people get it backward thinking they will be successful once they achieve great wealth. In order to achieve wealth, you must first focus on reaching success in your career, business, or whatever path you are following. Wealth will follow if you focus on the process of achieving your goals and creating a successful life.

Now It's Your Turn

Find a quiet place to contemplate your definition of success. Then write out your definition of success using the following worksheet in as clear and vivid a description as you can. This will be something you can formalize and post in a prominent place in your home or office to make sure you are on track to achieving the life you want.

If you are married or have a significant other, you should each independently fill out a worksheet. Then come together and discuss each list. This will help you to more clearly understand what you are each looking for and then determine how to define your success as individuals and as a couple.

> *"Always bear in mind that your own resolution to succeed is more important than any other one thing."*
> **– Abraham Lincoln**

Summary

Achieving success in life requires you to understand what success means to you. All of us, even the most successful people in the world, have self-limiting beliefs. These self-limiting beliefs get in our way of achieving success and cause us to hesitate and falter.

Self-limiting beliefs get in our way and block us from achieving the extraordinary coded into all of us. The first step in eliminating these beliefs is clearly defining what success means to you.

Do not be influenced by popular culture or by media images of what success SHOULD be. Success should be what YOU define it to be. Do not underestimate what you can achieve. You can achieve anything, but only if you have a clear vision of what it is you want and then take action. This includes removing self-limiting beliefs from your life and moving forward to get where you want to go.

When you consider what "success" means to you, identify those things you truly feel passionate about pursuing. There are many things that will catch your eye, but the truly important ones are those that also catch your heart. Be sure to include those things in your definition.

John James Audubon was unsuccessful for most of his life. He tried to be a good businessman, but no matter how hard he tried, he failed miserably. He tried changing locations, partners and businesses but it was no use. Eventually he began to understand that he needed to change himself in order to achieve real success. He made the decision to follow his passion. He loved the outdoors and was a good artist; he drew pictures of birds as a hobby.

Once he decided to stop being a businessman and started doing what he loved, his life turned around. He traveled the country watching and drawing birds. Ultimately his collection of art was collected and became a book titled *Audubon's Birds of America*. The book earned him a place in history as the greatest wildlife artist ever. Even more importantly, it gave him immense pleasure and satisfaction and the success he was seeking.

Decide what success means to you and what drives your passion. Once you have done this, you will have taken your first step to achieving unlimited success.

Exercise

Use the worksheet on the following pages to write your definition of success. Once you have completed it, set it aside for a day or two. Then come back to it and review what you have written. Make any required adjustments after you reflect on your definition. Take your time and put some thought into what you want from life. What you write here will determine the actions you need to take and the decisions you will make. Let your heart, dreams and desires guide you.

MY SUCCESS DEFINITION WORKSHEET

I have achieved success in my relationships when I ...

_____

_____

_____

_____

I have achieved success in my career or work when I ...

_____

_____

_____

_____

I have achieved success in wealth creation when I ...

_____

_____

_____

_____

_____

I have achieved success in power and/or celebrity when I …

_____

_____

_____

_____

_____

_____

I have achieved success in community when I …

_____

_____

_____

_____

_____

_____

I have achieved success in other areas of my life when I …

_____

_____

_____

_____

_____

_____

My additional measures of success are ...

_____

_____

_____

_____

_____

_____

Note: Do not feel that you must write something in every category above. What is important is that you fill in those areas that are important to you. Add or change categories as necessary to get your perfect definition.

CHAPTER 2

Creating Your Personal Vision Statement

"Vision without action is a daydream.
Action without vision is a nightmare."
— **Japanese Proverb**

Now that you have finished defining your personal version of success, are you ready to get started on your journey toward achieving it? The next step in your journey is to create a personal vision of what your success will look like when you achieve it. You must have a clear vision of who you need to be, what you need to do, and why you need to do it in order to achieve true success.

Now is the starting point toward your objective wherever you are in your personal or work life. Forget about the past and either build on the experience or change what you do in the future!

"I like the dreams of the future better
than the history of the past."
— **Thomas Jefferson**

Make a commitment to yourself that you will only look forward and keep your eye on your objective.

One of the great gifts we have as humans is the gift of choice. We have the capacity to make decisions and choices about our life and how we are impacted by the events in our life. We are affected every day by things that we cannot control; however, we can control our reaction to those things. Choose to make each day count toward getting what you want from life.

People often spend a lifetime seeking a purpose and meaning for their life's mission. By assigning your definition of success for your life, you have done just that. Your definition of success acts as your life's mission statement and is what should guide your thoughts, actions, beliefs and values. It is the reason you exist; the "why" of your life; a personal mission statement.

Converting Your Success Definition Into a Vision

In *Turning Your Dreams into Success*, Bunny and Larry Holman tell the story of Willie King and how he achieved his life mission even in the most difficult of situations. Willie had a very difficult childhood and at the age of 14, his father forced him to leave home. Willie lived on the streets at first and slept behind trash cans at night. Prostitutes on the street would come by to check on Willie to make sure he was okay.

Willie had a dream of what he wanted from life, what his mission was. So he stole raisin cakes to survive and took odd jobs to get by. As time went on, he found better jobs, and one day he happened to walk into a transmission shop looking for a job.

Seeing the owner struggling with a heavy transmission, he rushed over to help. He offered his time for free to the owner because he saw a chance to become educated on transmission repairs and take a step closer to his dream. As soon as he touched that first transmission, he knew that repairing transmissions was what he wanted to do.

Even through all his hardships, Willie knew what he wanted and drew pictures of his dream house on the wall of an old barn he was living in.

In 1994, he built that exact house on a seven-acre plot of land. Willie has owned several businesses and even though he has been through many challenges and obstacles along the way, he has overcome them all to achieve his definition of success. He is very involved in his community and leads or volunteers in several civic associations.

Willie believes that, while money is good, his community, people and the youth programs he is involved in are much more important. This is his vision of success, and his personal vision is to be a success so he can help others.

Willie has turned tragedy into triumph and has achieved true success in his life. He did it by taking it one day at a time and not letting obstacles stop him. He had a vision for his life, went out, and made it happen!

The search for fulfillment and happiness is as individual as each person is unique. Each of us has our own vision of success and our own ideas about how to achieve that vision.

Now you must take your personal definition of success and expand it into a personal vision statement. Your personal vision statement will address "what" you will accomplish from the success path you have identified. This vision will help you to begin to turn your success path into more concrete action steps that lead you to the life you want.

Shortly, we will identify the goals you will establish to help you define "how" you will achieve the success you desire. But first, you must have a very clear vision in order to decide what it is you want to accomplish. You may have very specific career goals in your definition of success, but the accomplishment of those goals ties into your personal success definition. In other words, the route you take to success must be as individual as your definition. There are no shortcuts.

There are times it will be difficult or things will happen that will challenge your commitment. If you remove the self-limiting beliefs holding you back and keep moving forward, you will be amazed at how much you can achieve and you will reach your destination.

You must begin to think of your life in different terms than in the past. Pretend for a minute that you are in an airplane flying home after a trip. As the airplane descends from 30,000 feet, you can begin to make out details in your hometown. At this height (on a clear day), you can see for hundreds of miles in any direction. There is very little detail and, in fact, all you see are the really grand features of our world, the mountains, large lakes, vast deserts and wide-open prairies and the lights of big cities.

As you get to 10,000 feet, you can see more clearly how the town is laid out; the patterns of the streets cutting the town into sections, lakes, golf courses, the downtown separated from the suburbs and all the other details that you miss when you are at 30,000 feet. From 10,000 feet, you get the big picture and can see things you may never notice driving around town. The first time you experience this it is pretty fascinating and it strikes you just how big and impressive your town really is.

As you continue your descent, things start to come into focus a little more. Now you can make out the cars on the street, some of the big billboards dotting the side of the highway, maybe some boats out on the lake, or a stadium full of fans rooting on the home team. The details are coming into perspective and the city is now starting to come to life. You still can see a fair amount of the city but less than you could at 10,000 feet.

Once you start coming in for the final approach and line up for your landing, you can see the people on the street, the vehicles are clearer and more details are coming into focus. After the plane has landed and you disembark the plane, you can see all the details. You now hear all the noises, smell the aromas and see all the details of the people, the buildings, etc.

The 30,000-foot perspective is the success definition. You should be able to see in your mind's eye the really big broad strokes of your life including all the things you will accomplish and what that will mean to you.

The personal vision statement is the 10,000-foot perspective. It will begin to tell you some of the details of how you will build the landscape of your life. You start to divide the really big world of your life into smaller more manageable chunks.

Once you have defined these manageable chunks, then we will move on to setting goals to achieve the "how" you will achieve each of the pieces that will lead to the ultimate definition of your success.

Critical Success Factors

Before you begin writing your personal vision statement, you must first define your critical success factors. A critical success factor is something that must happen in order for you to achieve your dream. By identifying these factors, you will be better able to understand what steps you must take and what goals to set.

Let me give you an example of a critical success factor.

Part of my definition of success involves helping as many people as I can through my work. I worked for nearly 30 years in the banking industry, and for the last five years or so, about the only real measurement of success that our sales team was given was how many checking accounts we could sell. We measured checking account sales in just about every way possible.

During all this time, I was in various leadership positions in the bank, but all of these positions involved sales management in some way. Every day I would wake up and think about how many checking accounts we sold yesterday and how many we would sell today.

This was NOT what I considered to be my definition of success for my career. In fact, I couldn't see how this corporate goal was anything more than pushing product. I would come home from work and complain endlessly to my wife about how this was not providing the meaning in my life I was seeking. So, in order for me to achieve my goal, I felt strongly that I would have to go into business for myself.

A critical success factor for me was to establish a nest egg that would support my family for at least a year while I invested in and built my own business.

In order to get to my 30,000-foot goal of helping as many people achieve their dreams and goals as possible, I had to establish a CRITICAL SUCCESS FACTOR that would allow me to get there.

My critical success factor became creating an investment portfolio large enough to allow me to go out on my own I knew how much I would need and would either need to save this, be able to borrow all or some of it, or have someone willing to invest in me.

Sometimes what we are doing today is leading us directly to where we want to go and other times we need to change the path. Critical success factors help you define what steps you need to take.

One of the greatest ways to reach your goals is to go into business for yourself and learn how to be successful at it. Today there are so many opportunities in the direct selling business or with franchises that help to lower the risk, making it impossible to ignore the opportunities available. If taking control of your career and earning potential is part of your definition for success, then you owe it to yourself to look into direct sales organizations and franchises.

Another critical success factor may involve the amount of time you spend at work. If part of your success definition is to spend more time with your family or to give more time to your church or community, then you need to have a critical success factor to work fewer hours.

How about possessions? What do you want to own during your life? Maybe part of success for you means owning a house, or moving to a certain part of the country, or buying a boat, traveling all over the world or owning a certain type of car. For some people it may mean how big of an airplane they want to own, how many vacation homes they want and where or how big the yacht will be.

To achieve the wealth you define for yourself (whether that is to retire comfortably or become a multi-millionaire), you may need to begin saving and investing – make that a critical success factor for you. You may need to make one of your critical success factors taking more risk in your investing or taking more risk in your life.

It doesn't matter what your dreams are, the important part is that they are *your* dreams and that you write down the details about what you are working to achieve. This will be *your* personal vision statement.

Exercise

Take a few minutes and list some of the things you need to do to achieve your ultimate definition of success. Don't worry about all the details at this point, instead focus on the bigger steps (the 10,000-foot view) you must take to arrive at your vision.

Your list of Critical Success Factors may look something like this:

1. Decrease the number of hours spent working without giving up on my career aspirations

2. Take more risk in investing to create more opportunities to build wealth faster

3. Improve my relationship with my spouse/family/ friends, etc.

4. Start my own business and take control of my own work success

5. Create enough wealth and passive income to support my family without NEEDING to work every day

6. Identify two or three ways to get involved and support my community with my time and/or money

7. Invest in more education, coaching, or other mentoring to improve my skills and make stronger, better decisions

You get the idea. Now it's your turn to create your list of Critical Success Factors.

_____

_____

_____

_____

_____

_____

_____

_____

_____

_____

_____

_____

_____

_____

Longevity of Your Vision Statement

While your definition of success will probably not change a lot over your lifetime, you may need to change your vision statement every three to five years depending on circumstances in your life. It is impossible to know what the future holds for any of us, so the vision statement may need to be modified to reflect the realities in your life.

Our personal vision statement is like the headlights on a car. It guides us to our destination by keeping us focused on what is ahead of us and where we are going. We would think nothing of driving from New York to California, leaving in the dark of night using our headlights. While we are driving, we are never really aware of what is going on ahead of us for more than a quarter mile at a time. There could be all kinds of delays, slow downs, detours, or maybe even an accident, but we trust that, as long as we stay on the road and follow the path we have chosen to take, we will reach our destination. At night, visibility is even more limited, but we proceed with confidence that our headlights will guide us.

Think of your vision statement as the directions you have mapped out to lead you along the roads of life to success. You may need to make a detour every once in a while, and you may even encounter an unexpected slow down or, God forbid, an accident. These events may force you to adjust your plan slightly but not the final destination. Choose to stay on course or make the necessary course corrections, map out your course, write them down and review them frequently.

Writing Your Personal Vision Statement

Hopefully, you have noticed that what you are doing is starting to create a plan for your success.

A written, well-defined plan is critical to arriving at the destination you chose for your life – without it, you will end up somewhere, but is it where you want to be!?

Your personal vision statement will be a document you refer to over the course of your journey. Refer back to your vision statement periodically as you move through your journey to make sure the path you are on is the correct one. If your vision is not leading you down the path toward your ultimate definition of success, then ask yourself why it is important to you and whether or not you should be investing your time in something that will not lead to your ultimate success.

Once you have determined that your goals are on the right track, then go after them with a passion and don't let anything get in the way.

To write your vision statement, use the worksheet at the end of this chapter. When you write your vision, you can either write it in paragraph form or in bulleted text, whichever will be easier for you to use. There will be multiple items covered, and you want your statement(s) to create a clear understandable picture of what success will look like. Listing the items in your vision in bulleted text may help you to keep them organized and clear. Be as clear and precise as possible, making it clear enough that anyone reading it will understand it without further explanation.

Write your personal vision statement in the "present" tense. Using the present tense activates the subconscious mind and helps you to lock your mental thoughts on making these events occur in your life. By activating the subconscious mind, you become alert to opportunities occurring around you that will move you closer to achieving your vision.

There is a Nobel Prize-winning theory about a group of cells at the base of your brain stem (about the size of a little finger), the Reticular Activating System (RAS), that serves as a small control center to sort and evaluate incoming data. Scientific research has established that the RAS filters out the urgent from the unimportant information so you can function properly.

An example of the RAS in action is demonstrated when you buy a new car. Have you noticed how it seems like every other car on the road is the same kind you bought? The reason for this is that your RAS has been activated. The type of car you bought is now loaded into your mind's control center and you notice the type of car you bought everywhere. It's not that there are more of them now; it's just that you now are programmed to notice them.

Imagine you are at a party, reception or similar event. The room is packed and you can barely hear the person with whom you are engaged in a conversation. Then, someone on the other side of the room says your name and that single word cuts through the noise and your ears immediately perk up. Again, that's the RAS at work.

Use your RAS to help you keep focused on the pursuit of your vision. By writing your vision out in the present tense, you help to lock it into your minds control center activating your RAS to help you achieve your goal.

Some of the vision statement(s) will be date or value specific. You may have a specific date in mind for when you will start your own business or when you want to achieve a specific title or position in your field of work. You may also have a date in mind to achieve a certain income level, for retirement or some other milestone in your life. Other parts of your statement will probably be expressed in more conceptual terms, such as relationships and spiritual needs. If you will need to improve your education or skills in any particular area, these may also be expressed conceptually as you may not know exactly what you need, only that you recognize you need more of it.

Example Vision Statement
The following are examples of things to consider including in your vision statement. You may also want to divide it into both

pre-retirement and post-retirement items. If you have other big life-defining events in your success definition, then you may also want to divide it into parts based on those life-defining issues.

Here are a few examples of items from my personal vision statement:

- I live a healthy and active lifestyle
- I work only with people with high integrity and honesty, coaching only those with a passion to succeed and a dream to chase
- Before age 55, we purchased our dream home on a lake with one or more acres of lakefront property
- We travel two or three times a year on vacation
- I work no more than 35 hours per week to maintain a balance between work and life
- Reach our financial target and cut back on my work hours to 20 to 25 hours per week starting at age 55
- I volunteer for community organizations and establish a foundation of giving
- Leave a legacy for each of our children that includes our charity work and financial support

You can see that these items support our previous definition of success as presented in our mission statement. Each item on the list fits into those dreams. The items I have listed here are not all that we have in our vision, but rather they help illustrate the process. You can make your list more descriptive and all-inclusive to make sure your vision is specific and clear.

Creating a vision statement will lead to the next step in the process of conquering your self-limiting beliefs – setting goals. Do not confuse this process with the goal setting process. They are very separate from each other, but you will take the vision statement(s) and turn them into specific goals that will lead you to the achievement of these visions that will get you to your ultimate success definition!

Exercise

Use the following worksheet to write out your personal vision statement(s). Refer back to the success definition (personal mission statement) you wrote at the end of Chapter 1 to make sure that your vision supports the mission of your life.

Refer back to your Critical Success Factors list as you compose your vision statement(s). These factors are vital to achieving your vision and ultimately your mission.

Compose your vision statement(s) and then set it aside for a day or two. Review and adjust as necessary after you have had a few days to think and reflect on the contents. Do this as many times as needed in order to make sure it is as clear, precise, focused and meaningful as possible.

Once you have done this, share it with someone you know and trust. Ask them for feedback. Do they understand what you are saying? Does it evidence there is emotion behind the writing and can they feel it come out in the statement(s)?

MY PERSONAL VISION STATEMENT(S):

CHAPTER 3

Go Big or Go Home

*"What great thing would you attempt
if you knew you could not fail?"*
— **Robert H. Schuller**

When was the last time you were convinced you could do anything you wanted and were completely unstoppable? As a child, you probably often felt this way. You did not think about failing; you did whatever came to mind and never worried about the consequences. In fact, you learned by failing!

As you learned to walk, you grabbed the table or a chair and pulled yourself into a standing position, then you let go and probably fell down. Of course, you were going to fall because you did not know how to walk! However, that didn't stop you from trying again, and again and again. The same was true with learning to read, write or ride a bike. We were unstoppable. Eventually you could do all these things automatically.

As we grow older, we begin to doubt ourselves and let the fear of failure or embarrassment slow us down. Our self-limiting beliefs about our abilities, our environment, our resources or ourselves get in the way and create doubt. These self-limiting beliefs tell us we are stoppable.

If you are to achieve your ultimate definition of success and create your vision as a reality, then you MUST remove these self-limiting beliefs. Don't let them hold you back and slow you down from achieving everything you want and are capable of in life.

> *"It is our duty as man and woman to proceed as though the limits of our abilities do not exist."*
> – **Pierre Teilhard de Chardin**

Go Big ...

> *"The greater danger for most of us is not that our aim is too high and we miss it, but it is too low and we reach it."*
> – **Michelangelo**

A fellow coach and good friend of mine taught me an important lesson when I first left corporate America to become an entrepreneur. My good friend Dawn Heartwell from Calgary, Alberta, Canada is a fellow coach and mentor who has inspired and helped me immensely in my coaching and as an entrepreneur. Dawn told me, "Dennis, go big or go home!" I've taken her advice to heart and have incorporated it into my life and my business.

After 29 years in a corporate job, I had achieved a high level of success within the industry. I rose to the position of a division president for a large regional bank and led several divisions within multi-billion dollar financial institutions. At one point, I was responsible for over a thousand people in my division.

Suddenly, the only employee I had was me! I was accustomed to managing a multi-billion dollar business and now it was just – me! My frame of reference went from big numbers and big goals to just hoping to earn enough to pay the bills.

I let my self-limiting beliefs get in the way. I still had the same personal mission (definition of success) and the same vision, but

I was thinking small now. Not for long though. Dawn set me straight.

I needed to start thinking in terms of what I wanted from life. According to Dawn I needed to start acting like there was nothing that was going to get in my way and go after what I wanted with passion and commitment. I had to choose to be great and not let my fears get in the way.

We all have in us the ability to achieve great things. In order to achieve that level of greatness we just have to get ourselves out of the way.

During an interview, Pro golfer Tiger Woods attempted to explain what happens when he gets ready to take a shot, "Sometimes I don't even remember hitting the shot. I remember pulling the club from the bag and standing over the ball, but the next thing I see is the ball taking off down the course. It's like I just get myself out of the way to make the shot."

Think of all the great things you could do if you just *got out of your own way*. In order to do this, you need to be willing to think and dream big. Don't let your self-limiting beliefs hold you back and create fear that gets in the way of your success. When you create your definition of success and your vision, you must be willing to set the bar high and stretch yourself.

... Or Go Home

Self-limiting beliefs will keep you from dreaming big. Life is meant to be enjoyed and to be fun.

"Man is born to live and not to prepare to live."
– Boris Pasternak

This book does not presume to tell you what to dream, but to encourage you not to limit your dreams just because of your fears. Don't let fear or self-doubt hold you back.

Go Big or Go Home means to dream big, set a fun, exciting, thrilling vision for your life and pursue it with all the passion you can find. If you're not willing to create a definition of success for your life that inspires passion in you then why bother?

Now is the time to start thinking big. In the space below, spend a few minutes dreaming. What are the big important things in your life you want to accomplish? Don't worry right now about "how" you would do these things but just dream about the possibilities.

My Dreams: _____

_____

_____

_____

_____

_____

_____

_____

_____

_____

_____

_____

_____

**Think big, dream big and take big action,
and you will get the life you want.**

Don't Settle

Be sure not to compromise on what you want to achieve in life. Dreaming allows you to consider the possibilities of what you can achieve. By writing out your dreams and checking them against your definition of success and your vision, you have opened up your imagination. Now, be sure that you don't settle for less than you truly want.

Too many times we allow ourselves to dream but then go back to our comfort zone. Don't let that happen to you now. Set the bar high on your dreams and be willing to go for it. Many people just settle for getting by and doing what it takes to survive. By taking the time to read this book, you have demonstrated a desire to achieve more out of life. It is important that you tell yourself you are no longer going to aim low with your dreams and goals.

Don't settle for anything less than everything you want from life. If you are tired of just settling for getting by and having a so-so life, you need to take charge and raise the bar. Raise the bar on your dreams to those things that you really want and stop shooting too low. Don't leave the quality of your life up to fate. It is your life so it is up to you to make it what you want it to be. The question is, "what will you make of it?" Will you achieve all that you want or will you let your fears and self-limiting beliefs rule your future?

Go back and review your definition of success and ask yourself; is my definition what I REALLY want out of life? Am I shooting too low or is this what I really desire to achieve? Are the dreams I have identified included in my definition?

Then look at your vision. Ask yourself the same question; am I shooting too low and is the vision I wrote exactly what I want my life to look like? If you find that – as you were writing your statements – you said something like, "what I really want is (blank), but I'll never achieve that so I guess I'll just put down (blank)," then you are settling! Make sure you included your dreams in your statements as well. Revise your statements and go for it!

It is critically important that you have real clarity about what you want from life before we move on. Take a few minutes and review your vision statements one more time. Make any final adjustments and re-write them again making sure you have not compromised on your dreams. If you have settled for something less than what you really want, then now is the time to change that. Don't settle! Use the worksheet at the end of the chapter if you need to revise your vision statement(s).

Your Dream Life

Remember, this book is about helping you overcome self-limiting beliefs and obtaining the life of your dreams. This is not a book about how to compile possessions or gain immense power. If those are your dreams then go for it; but that is not the main message.

Balance in work and personal time is more important than the things you own. History is littered with stories of people who pursued immense wealth and possessions and still were unhappy. Time with your family and time to enjoy your success is paramount to having the life you want. Living your dreams should not just be based on wealth and possessions.

The challenge to Go Big or Go Home is not a message about amassing money and things. The message is about defining your success as big as you want it to be in terms of ALL the things you desire. What do you want from your relationships, how much time will you have to enjoy your life and what legacy will you leave?

Ask these questions as you go back and look at your definition of success in Chapter 1. Then make sure your vision statements align with it. Think big and go big in defining the mission of your life.

A prime example is from the business world. Paula Deen has risen to become somewhat of a celebrity. But it didn't start out that way for her.

Paula was married at age 18, became pregnant at age 19 and lost both of her parents by age 23. A span of five years that had a major impact on her life. She became depressed and then severely agoraphobic. Agoraphobia causes someone to fear being in a situation where escape may be difficult or where help may not be available immediately, causing panic attacks and anxiety. For nearly two decades, Paula suffered from this affliction and barely ever left her home.

For those 20 years, she focused on cooking for her family and mastering the southern recipes her grandmother had taught her. By focusing on what was cooking in her pots, she was able to block out all the other thoughts causing all her anxiety. The process was therapeutic and provided her with structure and purpose to her day.

After consulting several sources, her salvation actually came from an unusual place – television. In 1989, she was watching an episode of *The Phil Donahue Show* where she finally learned the name for what she had been struggling with for so many years.

By this time, Paula had gone through a divorce and was forced to make a living for herself.

She set off on a journey armed with $200 and years of experience cooking and packing lunches for her children. So, she decided to make sandwiches and then sent her sons to downtown Savannah to sell boxed lunches to office workers. Every Thursday night she cooked into the late hours to create a mouthwatering Friday barbecue special, Boston Butt.

Her local specialties caught on quickly with the local business crowd and quickly became the talk of the town. In 1990, she opened a restaurant in the Savannah Best Western. The original restaurant was small and remained there only a few years before her core of faithful followers became too large for the small hotel restaurant. In 1995, she relocated to downtown Savannah and opened her now famous restaurant, The Lady and Sons.

Lady and Sons restaurant has won accolades from critics and the media alike. In 1999, *USA Today* honored Paula and her restaurant with the Most Memorable Meal of the Year award.

Paula is quoted as saying, "Now I'm done fighting and I'm done hiding." She made up her mind that she was not going to let her fears get the better of her and control her any longer. She set out to become successful and to use her talents and love of cooking to get there.

Today, Paula Deen's empire includes two restaurants, two television shows, five best-selling cookbooks and a biography, a cooking/decorating magazine, and a line of baking mixes and seasonings. Her popularity continues to grow all the time and she has been bestowed with the title of "Queen of Southern Cooking," by many of her fans.

Paula has achieved success in so many ways in her life, and her wealth and celebrity status is only part of it. She achieved success by overcoming her agoraphobia by taking ownership for what she needed to do to make her life the happy one she was looking for. She recognized that in order to succeed she needed to change and then proceeded to do it.

In other words, she chose to Go Big instead of going home and letting her fears control her. Once she made the decision to make something of herself doing the thing she loved the most – cooking – she didn't let anything get in her way. She went Big with her vision and with her goals and has become happy in the process.

You can do the same. Decide what success means to you and choose to Go Big with what you want to accomplish in your life and then follow your path to success without ever looking back.

Summary

Most people tend to dream too small and let self-limiting beliefs define life for them. Fate is not a good action plan for achieving your dreams. Don't settle for the small dreams that fear and uncertainty offer. Instead, raise the bar high and dream of the life you want. Close your eyes and visualize what life will be like when you reach your mission. Remove the doubt and the self-limiting beliefs from your thoughts, and you too, can discover the secrets of success.

"No pessimist ever discovered the secrets
of the stars, or sailed to an unchartered land or
opened a new heaven to the human spirit."
– Helen Keller

MY PERSONAL VISION STATEMENT(S) – REVISED:

CHAPTER 4

Writing Powerful Goals

"Write it down. Written goals have a way of transforming wishes into wants; cant's into cans; dreams into plans and plans into reality. Don't just think it – ink it!
– Author Unknown

By now I hope you are feeling good about your life mission and the vision you have created. You've given some serious thought to your future and can see in your mind the life you are ready to go out and get. It all sounds really good, doesn't it?

Now that you know your life mission and the vision you are going to follow, it is time to start working on the details of how to get there. How do you actually go from a vision to the accomplishment of your life mission? Remember, accomplishing your dream is a life journey.

Now that you have defined what success means and created a big vision, writing goals is a very critical step to making them a reality. Setting powerful goals is the next step in the process of achieving unlimited success. Setting concrete goals and then diligently working to achieve them is the only way to get you where you want to go.

Success does not have to be so complicated and difficult that achieving it requires great feats of super human effort. Warren

Buffett, listed as the second richest man in the world, is quoted as saying, "It is not necessary to do extraordinary things to get extraordinary results." However, without written measurable goals, life is a huge squirrel cage and you spend its precious seconds, minutes, days, months and years running frantically, in circles and getting nothing more than exhausted.

> *"Dost thou love life? Then do not squander time;*
> *for that's the stuff life is made of."*
> **– Aristotle**

Written goals are a critically powerful tool if you are on a specific path toward a very clear mission and vision. Written goals are the road you will follow to reach your vision. There will be milestones along the way to measure your progress, but you must follow the roads you mapped out if you are to arrive at your destination.

There is power in committing your goals to paper. Once committed to paper your thoughts are no longer imaginings; they are real. Ask any successful person if they have written goals; you'll usually get an enthusiastic Yes!

Studies have shown that only 3 percent of the population have written goals, and that group controls 97 percent of the wealth.

That is because these people have a clear path they are following and a way of telling if they are on track to achieve wealth and success. Amazingly 70 percent of people have NO written OR verbal goals or plans. If you want to achieve success and wealth you must have written goals.

The Common Misconceptions About Goals

There seems to be a misconception about goals. In business coaching I meet with many business owners who have worked incredibly hard for many years and are burnt out. Their business may be struggling to survive or they may have built a very solid profitable business, but the stress of it all is consuming them.

When I ask them about the goals they have set for themselves in their life and their business, more often than not, I get a blank stare. They often don't understand why they need to set goals. The responses typically are, "I'm just too busy to worry about things like that." "Goals are just a guess anyway so why do I need to worry about them?"

Many people seem to think that goals are just a guess and aren't going to change the results they get. They figure – if they just work harder – maybe things will get better and they'll start making more money or eventually be able to take some time off and go on vacation.

Let me give you an example of a discussion I had with a business owner. I met with Don in January 2006 to discuss issues he was having with the growth of his business; an auto repair shop. When I met with Don, it was obvious he was struggling to grow his business and was running up debt to keep the business open. He and his wife were struggling due to the stress this situation was causing them. In fact, the wife was not aware of the extent of the problem.

I asked Don what goals he had established for himself both personally and for the business. Don responded that he had no set goals other than to make enough money to pay his bills.

The conversation went something like this:

Dennis: "So Don, what are your profit goals for this year?"

Don: "I really don't have a specific goal; I just need to make more money."

Dennis: "Have you set a goal for your revenues for the year?"

Don: "No, I need to sell more than I am now; I know that much."

Dennis: "What is your long term goal for the business, say in 5 or 10 years from now?"

Don: "I really don't see any way I can stop working at this point but my wife and I want to stop working some day and do some traveling. I just don't know if we'll ever be able to do it."

This conversation went on for some time. I think you can see this is a person without a clearly defined mission or vision for their life. He doesn't know where he is trying to get to in life with enough clarity to understand what he needs to do to get there. In addition, because he doesn't know where he is trying to go, he doesn't see how goals will help him get there.

The common misconception that goals are just a guess and won't change the outcome is driven by the fact that people don't have a bigger end game identified for themselves. Without the mission and vision being clearly defined for your business and personal life, then you can end up setting goals that are not directed toward any specific path and can take you in the wrong direction. In fact, you just won't be able to see how goals can do much for you. The reason most people never reach their goals is they don't define them, or seriously consider them as believable or achievable.

Understanding the importance of having clarity about what you are aiming to achieve will change the way you look at goal setting. It will help you write powerful, meaningful goals that you are committed to. Your goals become a type of To Do list for the actions you must take to achieve your life's dreams. The more clarity you have around your mission and vision, the better you will be able to define what steps you need to take. Open your mind to all the possibilities and set powerful goals in line with your life's mission and vision. Doing so is a critical step to achieving success in life.

> *"An average person with average talents and ambitions and average education can outstrip the most brilliant genius in our society if that person has clear, focused goals."*
>
> – Mary Kay Ash

The Power of Having Your Goals In Writing

Why do your goals need to be in writing? Because having your goals in writing is non-negotiable to get you to your dream.

Some people are so clear on their purpose in life and what they want to achieve that they don't write down their goals. They can make the connection between what they are doing and how it gets them to the ultimate mission.

For most people that is not the case. Most of us need to have the power of the written word on our side. Once you commit it to paper it becomes real.

A goal not written down is just a dream!

While it is important to dream and use those dreams to guide your actions, they will remain dreams until you write them down and take action on them.

Once you have committed them to paper, your written goals will become the life you lead. Goals change how you think about things. If you change your thinking, then you change your view of the world. Your goals will change your thinking about who you are, who you can become and what you can achieve.

I have had goals almost all my life. I learned early that if I wanted to have the things I dreamed about then I needed to define what they were. Only then could I work on how I was going to get them.

I have always been a competitive person and wanted to be the best at what I did. In high school, I played the drums in just about every musical group I could find. I was in the school band, the marching band, the orchestra and the jazz band. I even played in my own garage band with a bunch of friends.

My goal when I joined the school band was to be first chair. For those of you never in band, the first chair is the person considered the best at that particular instrument. Players had to compete and try out to achieve first chair.

Now, gaining the top spot in the high school band's drum section doesn't seem like a big deal or even really that important. But, I can tell you that when you are 16 years old and involved in something with your friends, it feels important to be recognized as the best.

I decided if that was my goal I needed to determine how to achieve it. So I wrote down on a sheet of paper, "I will be the number 1 drummer in the Gahanna Lincoln High School band by the end of my sophomore year."

I then went on to decide what was needed to accomplish the goal. Taking lessons was one step and making sure that I practiced was another. I defined how much I needed to practice and spent extra time in the band room during study halls practicing the songs we were to play for the next concert. I took some of the songs to my private drum teacher and asked him to work with me on them.

I was the third chair the first time we tried out, but by second semester tryouts, I was named the top chair. I had a clear goal, wrote it down and kept it in front of me to remind me why I was practicing and stayed focused on it. When I got the results I wanted, there was a lot of pride that came with it.

Your goals do not have to be life altering or impossible to be effective. What is important is that you have a goal, write it down and then go after it.

Goals have been used by successful men and women in all walks of life. NBA superstar Michael Jordan tells how he visualized where he wanted to be and what kind of player he wanted to become. He says, "I guess I approached it with the end in mind. I knew exactly where I wanted to go, and I focused on getting there. As I reached those goals, they built on one another. I gained a little confidence every time I came through." Jordan set big goals and went after them. Think what we could all accomplish in our life and our business if we approached every day the same way he did!

Goal setting was very valuable to me in my career as well. After high school, I was hired at a local bank. I started at the lowest possible level in the company; I was the mail boy. I was the person that delivered mail to all the branches and the departments at our headquarters.

I could have decided this was a lame job and complained about it or given up and looked elsewhere, but instead, I decided to set a goal to be the president of a bank. Maybe not THAT bank but A bank.

I also knew that there was no way I was going from the mailroom to the corner office of the president directly. It was going to take at lot of learning, a ton of time and hard work to get there. So I set goals on what it would take to get there, and I started by writing them down.

It took hard work, a lot of learning and a lot of time – 23 years to be exact – but I did it. In 1999, I was hired as president of the Eastern Ohio region for the 21st largest bank in the U.S.

Some goals will come to you in a short time period and some are long term in nature. What is important is to have both long-term goals and short-term objectives. For now, it is important that you understand how critical it is to HAVE goals and to write them down. Turn them into something more than just vapor and dreams and make them concrete … in writing!

The SMART Formula

There is a common format used in many training programs and coaching programs for writing goals. The format is called the SMART format. It goes like this:

S pecific
M easureable
A chievable
R elevant
T ime bound

In order to make your goals come to life you have to make sure they meet the SMART test. If you simply write a goal in a very generic way then how do you visualize achieving it? How do you know if you are on track if you can't measure progress?

Let's go over each one and cover the importance of them individually.

Specific refers to making sure you are extremely clear on what it is you are aiming to do. You have to be as specific as possible and that means you need to visualize the outcome you want. What is the thing you desire? What result are you aiming for? Knowing the result you want and being as specific about it as possible in the goal setting process is the first step.

Measurable means that you will be able to measure your progress toward your objective. You can track where you are in the process and if you are moving in the right direction. Being able to measure your progress allows you to keep focused on the objective and correct your strategy as needed.

A goal must be **achievable** or why even write it? I wanted to be a bank president and felt very certain that goal was achievable even if it would take a long time to get there. But, let's say your goal is to become a multi-millionaire and you want to do it in the next month. Well, that might be possible but unless you are already well on your way to it now, that timeline is probably a little unrealistic. Don't make your goals so impossible that you can't possibly get there in the time you want and frustrated, you give up. That is the outcome that will occur if you set goals that are not achievable – you will simply give up.

A goal must be **relevant** to your overall mission to be effective. Ask yourself: Is this goal going to get me closer to my definition of success? There is no reason to set goals that will not move you closer to living the life you want.

The goal must also deliver a result to be effective. A goal should give you a defined outcome that you desire to achieve in order for it to be relevant. Do not write a goal as if it is the action step you need to take, but write it as the result you desire to achieve. Your action items will come out of your goals and should not be mistaken for the goal itself. To be relevant to your vision, make sure you are defining clear outcomes.

A goal that isn't **time bound** doesn't put any pressure on you to go out and take action. Set a date when this goal will be done so you can develop a plan to get there and then take action on the plan. The use of a timeline keeps you focused and on track.

> **You must set strong, impacting SMART goals to make them a powerful motivator to your success!**

How to Use SMART Goals in Your Life

Let's look at the SMART process in action. Let's say I set a goal to buy a new house. I could write a goal that says, "I will buy a new house for my family." In my coaching business, this is the kind of goal I run into all the time.

This goal is not very powerful. What type of house am I going to buy? Where will it be located? When will I buy it and how much will it cost?

Let's rewrite this goal using the SMART concept. It will now say, "I will buy a new home located in North Canton, Ohio in the St. James subdivision valued between $400,000 and $500,000 within the next 12 months. The home will have four bedrooms, two and one-half baths, a three car garage and be located on at least a one-acre wooded lot. It will be built of brick and have room for my family to grow."

Does this fit the model? It is very specific; you can almost see this house in your mind just by reading this goal. I can measure whether or not I have achieved it. It is achievable because I already own a home of similar value, and I can afford the purchase. There is a result attached and a defined time frame – less than 12 months. It is relevant to my long-term mission and vision and moves me closer to where I want to be.

You can see the difference between the two objectives and how the second one will help me stay engaged in achieving this goal. It is more effective because I can visualize it and it motivates me much more than the more generic one.

Make your goals SMART and make them meaningful to you so you can visualize them. If you want to buy a new house, go walk through a few new homes you would like to own and visualize yourself in it! If you want to buy a new car, go take one for a test drive and visualize yourself driving it! If you want a promotion at work, go talk to people doing that job and find out more about what they do so you can visualize yourself doing it. If you want to own a business, go talk to business owners and find out how they got started and see yourself in that role. The point is, if you have a specific personal or professional objective, you must dream it, see it and then write a very clear detailed goal for it if you want to achieve it.

Defining Your Goals

Your mission and your vision may extend out 20 or more years before you fully realize your ultimate definition of success for your life. It would be impossible to write one set of goals to cover everything needed to achieve ultimate success. There will be many things that come up during your journey that you cannot foresee today. Since your mission and vision may take many years to realize, you need to break your goals into shorter more manageable pieces.

Start by deciding what you need to accomplish in the next one to three years to get you moving quickly forward. What do you need to achieve during this time period to have a positive impact on your journey? Be sure to state these as SMART goals and stay focused on the outcome you desire. These goals will become intermediate milestones that help you measure your progress.

The process of goal setting is an on-going one. Each year you will review what you have accomplished, what you still have to do and make revisions as necessary. You will need to remain flexible and adjust to changing conditions in your life. By staying focused on the long-range goal of your definition of success, it will help you to stay on track. As you accomplish this first set of goals, you will be creating new ones that take you to the next level toward success.

One of your measures of success may be to create a passive income so you don't have to work, allowing you to enjoy the other things you want from life. But today you may be an employee in the corporate world. While you can't wait to get out of the corporate rat race, there will be steps you need to take before you can fulfill this mission.

Your one to three year goal could be to start your own business. Set a SMART goal to define what you want your business to be and when you will open it. There will be other goals that go along with that, like saving the money you need to get started, maybe debt reduction that needs to occur to allow you to free up capital, etc. These become the goals that tie into your mission and vision.

When writing your goals, don't overload yourself by assigning more goals than you can reasonably focus on. You will be living your life and dealing with all the day-to-day issues at the same time you are working on these goals. Ideally you should establish about five goals to focus on for the next one to three years. Since the goals are the outcomes you seek, they will focus on the larger achievements you need to attain. You will accomplish more by being realistic about how much you can do than by setting too many goals and becoming overwhelmed. Good goal setting will help you to focus on the right things that will have the biggest impact on your success.

Creating 90-day Objectives

Once you have established your first set of goals, use them to create short-term objectives of the immediate action you will take. These objectives will define specifically what you will do during the next 90 days.

This is a very important step because it gives you the immediate task list of what you must focus on. A 90-day time frame is manageable and allows you to become very specific with your action steps. Remember, it is the action that you take that will determine the results you will get.

This concept can be compared to the process you would go through to build a new home. When you make a decision to build a new home, it will probably take a year or more before you actually move in. The goal you set was to build a new home and you defined where it would be, how much you would spend and when you would do it. Once you have made that decision, there are a lot of intermediate steps you need to complete. During the first 90 days, you will need to get financing, pick out a builder, decide on a floor plan and style, decide on a lot to buy and so forth. Once those objectives are met, then you will start to pick out colors and make interior design choices. You may also be attempting to sell an existing home during this time. Those tasks may consume your second 90 days. The next 90- day period, there will be another set of objectives to complete.

This concept of building a new home is the same process you will go through to achieve your life goals. Set a one to three year goal, and determine what you will need to accomplish during the next 90 days to begin moving you toward that goal. Take the objectives you have identified that must be done, write it out and then go do it.

You may not accomplish everything identified for this 90-day period. If that occurs, then ask yourself if this is a real priority, and if so, what got in the way. Did you overcommit or did something get in the way? If you need to carry it over to the next 90-day period, then do so. If you determine that it is not really a priority, then remove it from your objectives.

Once you have completed those 90 days, set your plan for the next 90 days and do it again. This is a never-ending process and will lead to the ultimate success you desire. Our minds are built to think short-term and to concentrate on the task at hand. Setting objectives is the perfect way to keep you working on those things that will accomplish your goals.

From our example above, the short-term goals needed to start your own business might be to take some business courses. You might do some research on what type of business is right for you, researching franchises, direct sales organizations, etc. Setting some short-term objectives for debt reduction may be required as well as setting some savings targets. In order to be most effective, these objectives should tie directly to your goal of becoming your own boss.

As you accomplish your one to three year goals, you will reward yourself appropriately and then establish your next round of goals. After you have done this a few times, you will be amazed at how much you have accomplished and how much closer you are to the life you want.

Summary

Eliminate any self-limiting beliefs you have about goal setting. The most successful people in history have used the power of goals to get what they want from life. There is a lot of power in writing strong, meaningful, specific goals that you can post in a prominent place and review every day.

Remember, writing powerful goals and living them will change your world. You will become what you believe you can be and what you set your sights on becoming. Your destination to life success will be a journey and it will take many small intermediate goals to get you to the big one. If you want to achieve unlimited success, then writing powerful goals is absolutely critical. By setting precise goals and taking definite action, you will accomplish more in a year than most people accomplish in a lifetime!

Exercise

On the next few pages, list your goals following the SMART process. Start by listing the one to three year goals you need to achieve to get you moving toward your definition of success and the vision you have defined. Then take these goals and break them down into what you need to focus on for the next 90 days. You will need to refer back to the one to three year goals after the first 90 days to evaluate the progress you made and write your goals for the next 90 days.

"Your future depends on many things, but mostly on you."
– Frank Tyger

ONE TO THREE-YEAR GOALS
TO SUPPORT MY LIFE MISSION

Following the SMART formula, begin crafting your own goals.

S pecific
M easureable
A chievable
R elevant
T ime bound

Goal No. 1: _____

_____

Goal No. 2: _____

_____

Goal No. 3: _____

_____

Goal No. 4: _____

_____

Goal No. 5: _____

_____

MY 90-DAY OBJECTIVES PLANNER

Goal No. 1 (from page 68): _____

_____

During the next 90 days, I will accomplish the following toward long-term Goal No. 1:

1) _____

2) _____

3) _____

Goal No. 2: _____

_____

During the next 90 days, I will accomplish the following toward long-term Goal No. 2:

4) _____

5) _____

6) _____

Goal No. 3: _____

_____

During the next 90 days, I will accomplish the following toward long-term Goal No. 3:

7) _____

8) _____

9) _____

Goal No. 4: _____

_____

During the next 90 days, I will accomplish the following toward long-term Goal No. 4:

10) _____

11) _____

12) _____

Goal No. 5: _____

_____

During the next 90 days, I will accomplish the following toward long-term Goal No. 5:

13) _____

14) _____

15) _____

Note: Be sure to apply the SMART test to ALL of these goals. If it doesn't pass the test, revise it until it does and you will have a great plan to move you toward success.

CHAPTER 5

The 10 Most Common Self-limiting Beliefs

*"If you accept a limiting belief,
then it will become a truth for you."*
– **Louise L. Hay**

Before you identify the self-limiting beliefs specific to you, let's look at some of the common ones. Here are 10 very common self-limiting beliefs and what you can do about them.

The Top 10 Self-limiting Beliefs

I don't control what happens ... fate does

This is one of the most damaging yet common self-limiting beliefs in society today. How many people do you know that say things like, "I'm not lucky;" "if it weren't for bad luck, I'd have no luck at all;" "I have always been poor, and I'll always be poor" or "it's just not in the cards for me."

I'm sure you have heard many people say these things and you may have even said a few of them yourself. The reality is that fate does not control your success or failure. You do! It is that simple. You have to release from your mind any thoughts that fate and luck are the destiny of your future.

I certainly understand that some people believe there is a divine spirit that has a plan for our lives and that we were placed here for a specific purpose. I don't mean to say that this belief is not true. What I mean to say is that you should not limit yourself by saying that you cannot make the life you want because it is not your fate.

Your religious or spiritual beliefs should not interfere with how you go about achieving the success you want. You should not think you need to just take life as it comes and not try to create the life you desire.

You are in control of your future; however, things will happen in life that you do not control. You may experience an accident, illness or injury that impacts your current situation. You may have an unexpected layoff or downsizing at work or an unexpected tragedy.

While these can be devastating and consume your thoughts and time, they should not keep you from moving positively toward your goal. They may be detours on your way to success, but you cannot let them derail you.

Every day you must think positively and believe that you will reach your goals and dreams. Fate is not the master of your life and luck does not write your story. What you become and how you become it is your choice. Take positive action toward your mission and vision for your life, and you will find that the universe moves with you toward that goal.

Even if others think your fate should take you in one direction, you still need to decide for yourself what you want and forget about what others think fate has in store for you.

Jonah Wilson, the son of famous Beach Boy Carl Wilson, was on the fast track to success in the music industry. At the age of 19, Jonah became a road manager for a multi-platinum band, Wilson

Phillips. Two of the singers Wendy and Carrie Wilson are his cousins. Jonah says, "The music business was handed to me, but I wanted to create something for myself."

At age 21, he gave up the music business to pursue his vision for success and follow his dream in real estate. Jonah became a Real Estate Broker in Los Angeles and sold $50 million worth of property in 2005. It has taken him many years to get to this level of success. He says, "In the beginning there was fear, yeah. But if you want it, you want it. You fend for yourself and figure things out intuitively."

You need to decide what you will do with your life; fate shouldn't do it for you if you want to be truly happy.

There's not enough time

Sounds familiar doesn't it? How many times have you said that there just isn't enough time? Time is such a precious commodity in our life and yet we never seem to have enough time in our day.

> *"If time be of all things most precious, wasting time must be the greatest prodigality, since lost time is never found again."*
> **– Ben Franklin**

Time is the great equalizer. No matter how important or rich or famous you are, you still get the same amount of time as everyone else. We each get 1,440 minutes per day, 10,080 minutes per week and 525,600 minutes per year! I'm sorry to say that neither I nor anyone else can get more time for you.

It's not how much time we get, since we all get the same amount, its how we use the time that matters. Time management is a misnomer. We cannot manage time, the best we can do is develop the skill to not let time manage us.

The way to do this is to learn priority management. It is the priorities you set in your life that dictate how your precious time will be spent. So far, using this book as your guide, you have developed priorities for your life!

Your definition of success should guide how you use your time from a macro level. Your life vision will direct your priority management so you use your time to work on accomplishing the SMART goals you must accomplish.

When something is trying to take your time ask yourself, "Does this help me move closer to my goals and my vision?" If the answer is "yes," then you should invest the time and do it with passion and purpose. If the answer is "no," then you should not invest any time in it. It really is that simple.

Notice that I used the term "invest" instead of "spend" your time. It is important to recognize the difference between these. Normally when we talk about time, we use the consumption term "spend" when we should be talking in terms of "investing" our time, meaning that we are getting a payback when we do something.

The payback may be as simple as making your family happy or improving your health. It may be improving your knowledge or increasing the profits of your business. Time must repay you by getting you closer to your ultimate dream of success. Otherwise, if you just spend your time, you will never get that time back and will find yourself getting no closer to where you want to be.

It is completely up to you how to invest your time, but let me give you this advice:

Be absolutely BRUTAL with your time!

It's your life and your time. Don't let time manage you. Keep your definition of success, your vision of your future and your goals in a place you can review them often. Stay focused on how you choose to invest your time.

You must be brutal in how you ration out your time because no one else will do it for you. Take control of your priority management, and you will be amazed at how much progress you will make toward fulfilling your life mission!

I don't know how ...

In the Robert Kiyosaki book *Rich Dad Poor Dad*, he tells the story of a female reporter he met in Singapore. She requested an interview with him while he was there to give a speech. The reporter had a master's degree in English and was a professional reporter with a local newspaper.

She mentioned to Mr. Kiyosaki that she wrote novels and many people told her she was very talented. It was her goal to be a best-selling author and quit her job at the newspaper. She was discouraged because she wasn't having any "luck" (notice the reference to fate here) selling any books. She asked Mr. Kiyosaki for advice.

His advice was for her to take a class on sales and learn to become a great salesperson. Her reaction to this was to become furious with him and tell him that she was a professional and didn't want to stoop to the level of becoming a salesperson. She wanted to "sell" her books as her career but didn't want to learn how to sell.

This is a common problem that occurs all the time. What part of your definition of success and your vision do you not know how to do? It is important to identify the gaps between what you need to do to achieve success and what you currently don't know how to do to get there.

It is almost certain there will be some things you need to do that you don't possess the knowledge or skills today to do. This should not be a stopping point for your dream. All that you have to do to overcome this self-limiting belief is identify what the gaps are and create goals to overcome these gaps. Are there classes you need to take to gain specific knowledge or skills? Maybe you should take a part-time job or an internship with a company to learn skills you are lacking. Or it might be necessary for you to find a coach or mentor to help guide you.

Whatever the steps are, it is up to you to take the action required. If you are not sure what skills or knowledge you need, then do research. Talk to people in that industry, or conduct research. Information is available if you take the time to look for it.

> *"Determine that the thing can and shall be*
> *done, and then we shall find the way."*
> **– Abraham Lincoln**

At age 20 and without any business experience, Debbi Fields convinced a bank to finance an idea she had to open a business selling her homemade cookies. With no business experience at all, it would be safe to say that she didn't really know how – at the age of 20 – to build a company into a market leader in fresh-baked cookie stores. On August 16, 1977, Mrs. Fields opened the doors to her first Chocolate Chippery in Palo Alto, California. Since that time, the company has grown to over 900 company-owned and franchise stores with sales of over $450 million. If she had let the self-limiting belief that she didn't know how get in her way, then she would never have reached this level of success. Mrs. Fields didn't have the experience to accomplish so much success, but she found out how to create this amazing company and then did it. There were surely struggles along the way, but that did not deter her.

You, too, can take the steps necessary to create the life you want. As Mrs. Fields says, "You have to have passion when you're finding a recipe for a career. If you love what you are doing, you'll never work a day in your life." If you have that attitude, you will find it easy to do what you need to when conquering this self-limiting belief.

I don't have what it takes ...

> *"Whether you think you can or you think*
> *you can't ... you're right."*
> – Henry Ford

This is a very dangerous self-limiting belief. Telling yourself that you don't have what it takes is the same as shooting yourself in the foot. You are doing damage to your mind-set and your dreams in so many different ways.

You must remove the negative language from your life. If you tell yourself that you can not do something then guess what, you won't be able to do it. Your mental state says the task you are trying to do is not achievable, so you will convince yourself to fail or to not even try.

The mind is a very powerful tool and has amazing abilities to control what you can and cannot accomplish. I believe the quote above from Henry Ford is so true. If you think you can't, then you are right. You will not put your best effort into the task and you will find the universe aligning against you.

You can overcome this self-limiting belief, but the first step is changing your way of thinking and the language you use. Once you start looking at things from the positive mind-set you will be able to identify the steps you need to take. You will approach the solution with a winner's mind-set and attitude and accomplishing your goals will become much easier.

Eliminate from your vocabulary words like "can't," "don't," "won't," "not" and "no." These words create self-limiting beliefs whenever they are used. Stop telling yourself things like:

- I'm not skilled enough
- I don't deserve it
- I'm not sure I can do it
- I can't do it the right way
- No one cares
- I don't know how

There are many more we could list here but I'm sure you get the point. This type of thinking creates doubt, and the doubt leads to fear and fear leads to inaction. Take control of your thinking and change the negative language to positive wording.

- I can learn the skills I need to succeed
- I am deserving
- I have the confidence to do this
- I will learn the right way to do this
- People care how I am doing and if I succeed
- I will learn how

If you keep telling yourself what you CAN accomplish instead of what you can't, you will find that your attitude and beliefs change. You will approach your day and the actions you take to achieve your goals in a more positive mental state, and tasks that once seemed intimidating or impossible are now doable.

> *"All that we are is the result of what we have thought."*
> **– Buddha**

If you are in the position where you don't know how to do something on your 90-day objective planner, or on your vision statement, then tell yourself you will take the steps to figure out how to do it. Say, "I will learn how to …," and then ask for help from a mentor, read a book, take a class, research it at the library or on the internet or anything else you need to do.

If I only work harder … (hard work is noble)

Have you ever worked in a company where your value to the organization was measured by how hard you worked or how many hours you put in? When did we, as a society, decide that working really long hard days became a measure of success? In many companies, taking a vacation can be seen as a weakness or lack of commitment to the company.

I worked in the corporate world for 29 years and saw a real shift over those years toward encouraging employees to work unreasonably long hours and demanding more and more from them all the time. The concept became known as "doing ever more with ever less."

As I moved up the corporate ladder, the demand became even greater. Sure, I was making a lot more money, but I really struggled to find the time to enjoy it.

At one point in my career, I was given a Blackberry and told I was expected to use it to check email and keep in touch seven days a week. If an email was sent to me at 11:00 pm or on a

Sunday, I would be questioned about why I didn't respond right away. These certainly weren't life altering messages and a quick reply was not required, but was expected.

During that time, I believed that unless I worked 60+ hours a week and made myself available at all hours of the day to my job, then I wasn't pulling my weight. It didn't matter how good the results were. Even if you got great results and didn't need to work exorbitant hours to do it, you were still expected to "work hard."

In my coaching business, I've talked to hundreds of business owners and a common theme is they work long hours and have very little leisure time. It is a common belief if you own your own business you are supposed to work long hours. What occurs is the business owner becomes consumed with the business, and before you know it, they are burned out and frustrated. Owning the business is no longer fun and they begin to feel trapped and don't know how to change.

Hard work is ok and working long hours is fine as long as it does not become a habit and consume your life. In order to achieve success, you may need to work some long hard hours. That is a fact. But, don't allow your belief that you need to work hard impede your progress toward your definition of success.

Don't confuse working hard with making progress toward your goals. Being busy does not necessarily mean you are getting closer to success.

It is not how busy you are that will determine whether you succeed or not. It is what you do with your time that matters. Make sure the work you are doing is meaningful and is focused on the goals you have decided will lead you to success.

Remove from your beliefs the idea that you must work 50, 60, 70 or more hours each week to succeed. If you are working for a company that expects this of you, go talk to your boss. What is important to the company; achieving the objectives they have given you and making a contribution to the company or working long hours? If you can be a valuable member of the team and still have time to work on the other goals in your life, then do it.

The other choice is to investigate the idea of starting your own business and controlling your own time. If you build your company correctly from the beginning, you can control your time more effectively than working for someone else. It will take some hard work to get it started but the rewards can be great. There are many opportunities in the direct sales (also called network marketing) industry and in franchising that can get you started.

People like you have real lives and real responsibilities – kids, houses, debt, bills – and you can't just quit your job and go out on your own. You can start part-time, maybe working evenings or weekends to get started until you build enough income and momentum to go full-time in your own business.

The concept of direct selling or a home-based business is very appealing. For more than 50 years, direct sales companies have provided opportunities for men and women to start taking control of their own success.

Today there are hundreds of these types of companies in industries such as homecare, personal care, health and fitness, skincare, clothing, jewelry, financial services, pet care and the list goes on. Direct selling accounted for over $30 billion in sales in 2005 with over 14.1 million people involved in selling these products. These types of opportunities have created thousands of millionaires over the years.

These as well as franchise opportunities can create lifestyle businesses that won't require you to work extremely long hours to succeed if they are managed correctly. You can also develop a business plan and start a business from scratch. There are so many great success stories of people who have taken a new idea and created a very successful business.

Determine what will best help you achieve your ultimate success and then follow that path. Whether you choose to start your own business or work for someone else is less important than making sure it fits in to your success definition.

Overcoming the self-limiting belief that achieving success is going to be "too hard" is important if you are to accomplish what you want in life. By developing a plan and putting it in writing, you have taken a major step forward. Nothing is too difficult to accomplish if you set your mind to it and stay committed to it. If your definition of success and your vision are truly what you want from life, then pursuing them should not feel like work. Instead, they should inspire you and motivate you. It may require you to put in extra time early on in the process and to stretch your knowledge and skills. Knowing what you are going to achieve should make it all worth it.

Blame, Excuses and Denial ...

What was your favorite excuse when you were growing up and you did something wrong? When your Mom wanted to know what happened, you were probably quick to have some type of blame, excuse or denial for it. Maybe you told your Mom your sister did it, or it wasn't your fault; the wind must have blown the lamp over and broke it.

When we were young, it was easy to come up with reasons why things weren't our fault. Our Mom and Dad might not have believed us but that didn't stop us from trying. If you have ever lived with a child in your home (especially a teenager), then you know what it's like to have someone always coming up with excuses. I've raised three wonderful children and I've heard about every possible excuse imaginable. I forgot, I was too tired, Mom didn't tell me, my alarm didn't go off, the teacher never taught us that, the teacher doesn't like me, and the list goes on and on.

Blame is also favored by children. There is always someone to blame when something doesn't get done, is broken, or didn't work out the way it should. As parents, we tend to get blamed for everything wrong in their life or anything that didn't get done right. It is actually comical sometimes the extent they will go to in order to find a path back to something their parents did that caused the problem – because it surely couldn't be them!

Even as adults, we still can come up with reasons why things aren't our fault. How many times have you ever blamed others for not getting what you want? Maybe it's due to your boss, the economy, your customers or co-workers, your employees, your competitors, etc.

It is so much easier to believe it is someone else's fault when we fall short of achieving success, but the truth is all you are doing is giving yourself an easy way out. You are letting yourself off the hook.

The people who complain the loudest about never having an opportunity in life are usually the ones who always have an excuse for their failures. Nothing is ever their fault as they are always victims of their environment, circumstances or any number of factors. If you try hard enough, you can always find a reason for not attempting something in your life or not staying with it to the end.

**You are denying the reality of the situation
to give yourself permission to fail.**

Successful people are not excuse makers. Instead, they take responsibility for their actions and for achieving what they set out to do.

There is a poem I really love that speaks to the self-limiting belief of wanting to blame others or circumstances instead of taking responsibility for our actions, decisions and results.

Pursue the Passion
by Michelle True
www.michelletrue.com

Why are passions not pursued?
Because we just aren't in the mood,
or do not think we have the time,
or find the ladder too steep to climb.
There's always something, someone else
to blame for passions on the shelf.

Covered with dust, we watch them die;
there's always a perfect alibi.
A demanding job, long hours, the kids,
the success a part of us forbids.
Just living day to day must do;
to lofty dreams we bid adieu.

We don't think we deserve to dream
yet deep inside our passions scream,
desperate to be set free.
Ideas born in reverie
languish, cob-webbed in our mind.
To failure we've become resigned.

We conform to the status quo,
with no opportunity to grow.
We quietly follow the herd,
our passion and our vision blurred.
Are we simply too damned tired
or are we no longer inspired?

We never broke free from the mold,
no longer reaching for the gold.
Our hopes to one day be fulfilled
have somehow, silently, been killed.
We find success others defined,
our dreams falling further behind.

We're lacking proper motivation
or simply lost the inclination;
postponed dreams to a later date
while silently, we moan, berate
our lack of progress, sitting still.
We feel no joy; there is no thrill.

Our dreams slip slowly from our grasp
not uttering a single gasp.
Taking such a loss for granted,
we forget the seeds once planted.
We have the power to evolve
but lack the strength and the resolve.

There is no adequate excuse.
It is a form of self-abuse
to deny ourselves what we deserve.
Have we only lost our nerve
or has it fallen out of fashion
to actively pursue our passion?

Life happens! That is just a fact. There is no doubt that sometimes things happen that are out of our control. While we can't always control everything that happens in our life, what we can control is how we react to it.

Kay Yow, coach of the North Carolina women's basketball team, recently won an ESPY award. During her acceptance speech, she described how she has dealt with her battles with cancer. This is her third battle with cancer and all the treatments that go along with it. While it would be natural for her to have a "why me?" attitude, she instead had a very positive outlook on life. She explained how the experience has given her an opportunity to teach and coach her players and assistant coaches about the value of attitude. She could have chosen to use blame or excuses to keep her from performing well or staying focused on helping her basketball players be their best. In fact, she took her team to the NCAA Women's Tournament while fighting the disease. Her inspiring story shows what is possible if we stay focused on what we can control in our life and work through those things that are not in our control.

It is quite natural for us to focus on the challenges we face and how those challenges impact us. But, it is more important for us to focus on the outcomes we want instead. By focusing your attention on what you do want instead of what you don't want, these challenges will not become deterrents to your success. The impact of facing your challenges head-on with a positive attitude will have a major impact on what you achieve in life.

Your responsibility is to not let yourself take the easy way out by saying the problem or lack of progress toward your goals is not your fault. Whether it is or isn't doesn't matter. What matters is that you recognize the problem and then deal with it. You must choose to respond to it by taking ownership of the problem and looking for a solution.

To overcome this self-limiting belief, you need to identify there is a problem, explore why it happened and take responsibility to fix it. If you choose to stay focused on a positive outcome and not let the setback or problem get you down or derail you from your pursuit of success, you may still have a temporary setback but it will not stop you.

I'm afraid of failing ...

> *"Winning means being unafraid to lose."*
> **– Fran Tarkenton**

The fear of failure is so strong in all of us that it becomes a major self-limiting belief. This self-limiting belief alone has kept many people from pursuing their dreams of success. We are taught all our life that failure is a bad thing.

Let's get this straight right at the beginning ... .

Failure does not have to be a bad thing! Although we often believe that failure is the direct opposite of success, it isn't. Failure is a great teacher along the path to success.

In fact, almost every truly successful person has failed several times during their life. In some cases, the failures were spectacular, huge failures that led to the loss of a fortune and maybe even bankruptcy. But in most cases, the failures are setbacks not catastrophes.

We have all heard that Thomas Edison had thousands of 'failures' while he was trying to invent the incandescent light bulb. After thousands and thousands of attempts, he finally found a way to make it work. When asked about his failures, Thomas Edison is quoted as saying, "I have not failed. I've just found 10,000 ways that won't work."

We all make decisions in our life requiring us to face possible failure. In fact, I would argue that every big decision you make has that risk inherent in it.

The decision to get married has the risk of creating a failed marriage. There is risk inherent with the purchase of a home due to the risk your income will change and you won't be able to pay the mortgage. The same is true with making an investment; you don't know if it will pay off or flop.

Career decisions are the same way. Do you leave your current job to work for a different company or to start your own business? Starting your own business certainly has the risk of failure. If you move to another company, what if you just fail at the new job or you don't like it?

You may not analyze every decision this way, but we all tend to stop and think twice about the big decisions before we act. I've faced these same choices. In 1993, I was a regional vice-president for Household Bank. We lived in Ohio at the time where I had spent all my life. I had spent my entire banking career to that point working in branch operations, sales and lending.

One day my boss offered me a big promotion. He wanted to promote me to the position of national director of training and development for the bank, the mortgage company and the operations company. This meant I had to move my family to Chicago!

The emotions were very mixed about the opportunity. This promotion would move me one step closer to my initial career success goal of becoming a bank president. Taking this position would give me experience running a corporate level function for the company. It would also give me exposure at all levels of the company in addition to stretching my leadership skills and teaching me new skills.

Given all the positives of the promotion, why wouldn't I accept it? Well, let me tell you, there was a lot of fear with this decision. The obvious first fear was we had to move to Chicago and leave behind everything we knew. Moving a family to an unknown city was very difficult and a little scary since we had never done it before.

Add to that the risk associated with the promotion itself. I knew very little about creating, developing and delivering training programs. I would be leading the needs analysis, instructional design, delivery and quality of all our training programs. Plus, I would need to interact with the directors, presidents and CEO's of various divisions and corporate businesses.

There was certainly the chance of failure in this role. I would need to work hard to gain credibility, develop new skills and demonstrate the leadership necessary to succeed. If I failed, then what? I would be starting over in a new city away from everything I knew.

I made the decision to accept the risk and moved to Chicago. I performed well in my new role and things were looking good. We settled into our new home and made a nice life. I was confident in my ability and accepted the rewards would be greater than the possible failure.

But that's not the end of this story. Although I believed in myself and felt confident in our decision and our ability to settle in the new city, some of the risk was simply out of my control.

Approximately eighteen months after we moved, the holding company for the bank, Household International, hired a new

CEO. The new CEO made a quick decision to exit the retail banking business and sold or closed virtually all the divisions and departments for the bank. As you might guess, my position was eliminated!

Even if you do sufficient research and have all the confidence in yourself, there are still risks you cannot anticipate. That does not mean you should be afraid to act. Quite the contrary, you need to gather the facts; analyze how the decision you are about to make impacts your long-term personal success definition and personal vision. If the decision supports your journey toward success and the facts tell you it is a reasonable risk, then go for it. Don't let your fear of failure keep you from acting … you can't control all the variables anyway.

What you can be certain of is, you will NOT achieve your goals if you let fear get in the way.

Normally what we fear does not actually happen. Fear is usually in our mind more than it is a reality. We tend to fear what we do not understand or what will cause significant change in our life.

Failure is an important step toward success. Most people operate in the mental mode that puts them in the middle with success on one side and failure on the other. They do everything they can to move toward success while moving away from failure. But, we learn as much – and sometimes even more – through our failures.

After my position was eliminated with the bank, there was about 30 days of uncertainty before a new opportunity opened up in the company. It was an avenue that did not exist previously. I took the new position as senior vice president of our newly formed direct bank. This opportunity taught me a whole new set of skills and allowed me to move more quickly toward my goal.

My path was altered slightly but I still achieved my goal to become a division president. It was with a different bank but that was okay. By staying flexible, believing in myself and not letting the fear of failure deter me, I reached my goal.

You can do the same in your life. I carried the lessons I learned through this experience into starting my own coaching business. I have applied them in my business to keep me moving forward even when there were times that failure was possible. To once again quote Thomas Edison,

> *"Our greatest weakness lies in giving up. The most certain way to succeed is always to try just one more time."*

Starting a business is a very risky enterprise. Eighty percent of all new businesses fail within the *first* five years. Eighty percent of that remaining 20 percent fail within the *next* five years. Ninety-six percent of all businesses won't make it to their tenth anniversary. Why do so many fail? A major reason is the lack of a plan and the will to face the fear of failure.

Those that do make it have had failures – of varying degrees – along the way. But they persevered, didn't give up on their dream and accepted failures as learning experiences to help them grow stronger.

Create your plan using the steps in this book then take action without letting the fear of failure get in your way and you will achieve success. As small failures occur along the way, welcome them, embrace them and learn from them. Instead of viewing failure as something to be avoided, turn it into a stepping-stone on the path to success.

If you keep a strong positive mental attitude, you will not see these failures as proof of your inability to succeed. You will see them as positive proof that you are taking action, learning and growing as you take your journey toward earning the life you want!

Don't let fear paralyze you and keep you from taking the steps you need to accomplish what you dream. It is your life and you are the one who needs to take action to get what you want. No one else is going to do it for you, and it would be a shame not to have the courage to get what you want.

> *"Courage is fear holding on a minute longer"*
> **– General George S. Patton**

Don't let fear be the reason you don't get what you want from life. Remove this self-limiting belief from your thinking and have the courage to pursue your dreams.

Wealth and success are for others ...

> *"Nothing can stop the man with the right mental attitude from achieving his goal; nothing on earth can help the man with the wrong mental attitude."*
> **– Thomas Jefferson**

Complete the first four chapters of this book writing out your personal success definition, your personal vision statements and your goals. What do you think would happen if you went into work tomorrow and told five people that you just finished defining success, writing out a personal vision and setting goals to accomplish success?

I'll tell you exactly what would happen. Four of those five people would look at you like you were crazy and the fifth one would admire you for doing it. They might even try to tell you it was a waste of time. They would say, "you don't really believe that stuff will work do you?" A few might even wonder why you thought you were so special that you felt you could achieve some lofty definition of success. The doubters and nay-sayers would go on and on about why you were crazy.

There will always be those that believe they don't control their life. Wealth and/or success are for others and not for them. You are not one of those people! The fact you picked up this book and have made it this far is proof you understand that you get out of life what you think about, plan for and take action to achieve.

Everyone has the ability to achieve the life they want. But first, they must define it and be willing to take positive, focused action to get it.

Fred DeLuca graduated from high school in 1965 and wanted to attend college but couldn't afford the tuition. In July of that year, he attended a reunion for a friend, Dr. Peter Buck, who was moving to New York. Fred decided to ask Dr. Buck for a loan to pay for tuition.

Dr. Buck instead offered to invest in a submarine sandwich shop with Fred telling him that if he opened the sandwich shop he would earn enough money to pay for college. Fred was very surprised by his offer but decided to take him up on it.

Fred opened the sandwich shop and ended up on a roller-coaster ride that turned his sub shop into Subway Restaurants. Success for him required learning a lot of new skills and perseverance, but through it, he achieved financial success and everything that goes along with it.

Fred achieved success and he had no more right to it then you or me. I have seen some people almost refuse to accept success because they have a self-limiting belief that has built up over a lifetime of not getting what they want.

As a coach, I see some business owners with the self-limiting belief that their business is doomed to mediocrity. They are accustomed to seeing poor to average results. When the business begins to succeed in a bigger better way, they are afraid to accept that the success is real.

One client I have worked with experienced a 358 percent increase in profits in the first year of coaching. Revenues were up and the leads coming into the company were steadily increasing. To my surprise, it took the owners quite a while to accept the new levels of success. Years of achieving mediocre results created a self-limiting belief about their company's ability.

How has your past experience defined your self-limiting belief about success? Have you been unhappy with the results you have achieved in your career or with your business? A recent *USA Today* survey indicates that 53 percent of people in the American workplace are unhappy with their current job. That is very disturbing and raises the question, what are they doing about it?

Whether you like or hate your current job, the important thing is that you take control of your life by taking whatever action is needed to move you closer to success. It may require you to make some changes in your life, job or business. Now that you have clarity about what you want, you can begin to make those changes. Believing that you deserve success is important to making those changes.

Anyone can achieve success and wealth if they are willing to take the necessary steps. In order to abolish the self-limiting belief that wealth and/or success is for others, you must first change your thinking and visualize daily what you are trying to achieve. Keep your personal definition of success and your personal vision statement in a place where you can review it frequently. Visualize you achieving your success and taking the steps required to get there. Then don't let anything get in your way of making it a reality.

It is absolutely true that nothing on earth can help the man/woman with the wrong mental attitude. Change your attitude and you will change your world. Success is sure to follow.

This is going to be too hard ...

> *"The man of fixed ingrained principles who has mapped out a straight course and has the courage and self-control to adhere to it, does not find life complex. Complexities are all of our own making."*
> – B.C. Forbes

The year was 1970 and I was just entering junior high school. I was starting sixth grade and I always loved football. My parents never really encouraged me to play on an organized team, but I wanted to play on the school team.

I went to the coach's office to find out what I needed to do to join the team, and I ran home to tell my Mom about it. When I got home and told my Mom, she didn't seem overly excited about it (I think she was afraid I would get hurt). She told me how hard it would be. I would have to practice every day, I would be sore all the time and might even break some bones or something.

After talking to her, I started thinking about how hard it would be and how much time it would take. I never went back to see the coach or attend a practice. At that early age, I talked myself out of joining the team and playing a game I absolutely loved because I thought it was going to be hard work.

Many times I have looked back on that decision and truly regretted it. I never played on an organized football team. I played on basketball teams, track teams and other sports but never football. There's nothing I can do about it now. It's too late!

Many of my friends joined the team and had a great time. They loved playing and went on to play for several years. Why could they do it and not me? I ask myself that question sometimes.

How many times have you avoided doing something because you thought it would be too hard? We have all faced challenges and will again as we pursue our goals. But, just like my example above illustrates, most if not all of the obstacles are ones that we create in our mind. I didn't play football because, in my mind, it would take too much time, be too demanding and I might get hurt.

The same thing happens in our business life. We look at the people holding the executive positions, or the business owners that have made a lot of money and wish that was us. In my business as a coach, I continually see a huge disparity between the success levels of companies in the same industry.

As an example, the landscaping industry in my community has many competitors. Three of these landscaping companies dominate the local market and, then there are a lot of small companies struggling to survive. I have talked with owners of both the struggling and the dominate companies and it is easy to see why some are doing better than others. So much of it has to do with the owner's mind-set and how they approach the business. The owner of the struggling company says he is way too busy to attend a workshop, hold a meeting with me or work on plans for the future. This owner is so busy working in the business every day doing the landscape work that they never stop to plan how to make it better. He tells me it will be too hard for him to find the time or energy to do the things he needs to do to succeed, and if he just works harder, maybe things will get better.

Contrast that to the owner of the large successful landscape company. The owner of one of the top three attended a recent workshop I held on how to improve your business. I began talking to the owner and learned that he makes it his goal to attend at least two or three such events every year. He believed that if he picked up even one idea he could use to help his business, it was a great investment of his time.

He asked me to meet with him and his partner to talk about their business. Over the next few weeks, we spent a couple of hours talking about the business; what his plans, goals and dreams are for it and the things that he felt they needed to improve.

I learned that – only three years earlier – he had been a much smaller company. But, he had made it his priority to learn how to make the business a bigger success and create wealth. He understood the importance of being brutal with his time and investing it, not spending it. He understood that asking for and getting help was a great thing and not a sign of weakness. He did not let the fear of failure get in his way even though there were times he felt he may not make it. He also knew that you need to continue to learn and grow no matter how successful you may already be. He recognized that success required him to invest his time on the right activities.

Now, three years later, his business is flying and he is creating amazing wealth for himself and working fewer hours. The business can run without him for extended periods and he is free to pursue other activities if he chooses.

If you are an employee working for someone else, the same principles apply. If you want a promotion, or to change careers, or to become a better salesperson, or to leave your company and start your own business, it is up to you to determine what it is going to take to get there. You must be willing to accept the fact that you may need to re-set your priorities to gain the skills, knowledge and support you need to make it happen.

You can use the excuse that you lack the time or resources to get the support you need and develop the skills required to get the success and wealth you want. Or you can eliminate those thoughts from your mind and tell yourself you are going to do whatever it takes and get busy doing it.

The self-limiting belief that this is going to be too hard requires you to change your thinking. It may be hard at first, but if you pursue the plan that you set out for yourself, re-set your priorities about how you invest your time and keep focused on your goal, you will find that it gets easier with time, and you will end up with the life and happiness you desire.

It will only truly be hard if you don't have a plan to follow and the desire to get there. The only complexities in life are the ones we create for ourselves.

Define success, create a vision, set your goals and then believe with everything in you that you will get there. Be brutal with your time, invest it wisely and get the help and support you need, and your path will not be nearly as hard as you think. Your life is yours to make, make it the one you want!

I'm not a salesperson ...

> ### *"Everyone lives by selling something."*
> **– Robert Louis Stevenson**

When I say salesman to you, what is your first reaction? Grab a piece of paper and a pen and draw a line down the middle of the page. In the left column write all the negative thoughts you have about salespeople. In the right hand column write all the positive thoughts about salespeople.

Which column is longer? If you are like most people who attend my workshops, then the left column is much longer. Even if you are in sales you probably had more in the negative column than the positive one. Why is that?

We have all had negative experiences with sales people at some point in our life. Most people really hate to be sold anything. Our defenses come up immediately when we are approached by a salesperson in a store or when we get a phone call from someone trying to sell something.

You may be wondering what this has to do with you. Your definition of success, your vision and your goals might not have anything to do with being a sales person, right?

Wrong! This self-limiting belief is one most people have, but they don't recognize how it affects them.

> **It doesn't matter what your dreams or goals are, they involve sales of some type. We have to sell everyday of our life whether we realize it or not.**

Let me give you an easy example. The other day I had about an hour between meetings with clients, so I decided to stop off at a local restaurant for some breakfast and to spend a few minutes working on this book.

The waitress didn't greet me for several minutes, and when she finally did, she did so by holding a coffee pot in one hand and – as she walked past – looked over her shoulder and said, "Coffee?" I said, "no" and started to say that I wanted tea instead, but she heard me say no and just kept on walking.

After a few more minutes, she returns and takes my order including, finally, my tea order and disappears. I was busy writing when she returned a few minutes later with my order. Instead of saying anything, she just set the plate down on top of some of my work papers said, without much enthusiasm, "you need anything else?" and walked away.

She was not really nasty or mean to me. The food was good and it arrived quickly and she cleared the table promptly. However, when it came time to leave her a tip, I left her about half of what I would have left her if I had liked her. Did you get that last part, *if I liked her*? You see, she was selling me her service, and I was going to pay her what I thought it was worth.

She probably never thinks of it like that and wonders why she doesn't get the tips she thinks she should. She probably blames the cheap customers or the lousy restaurant owner. But the truth is she didn't sell me well enough to make what she could have.

Are you married or do you have kids? Then you are selling to them every day. You may need to sell kids on why it is important to get good grades, why they shouldn't take drugs, how to be good citizens, etc. You need to sell your spouse on why you should or shouldn't spend money on a certain purchase, why they should take you out to dinner tonight, or why you should take that big promotion at work that will require you to move the family. If you want to start your own business, then you will have to sell a lot of people to make it a reality.

If you are an employee, you will be selling your boss on why you are a good employee, why they should keep you employed, why you deserve a raise or promotion, etc. If you own a business, then you need to sell your employees on why they need to be good employees, your customers on why they should do business with you, your banker on why they should lend you money and the list goes on and on.

To succeed in life, you MUST be a good salesperson! You must overcome any doubts or fears you have about sales and learn to embrace selling as a way of life.

Now please, don't let fear of sales cause you to close this book and stop here. It's not that you have to learn how to sell used cars or real estate or even widgets. What I am talking about is learning how to sell your ideas, your dreams, your skills and your knowledge to accomplish what you want.

You need to understand how to persuade other people to give you opportunities to do the things necessary to learn new skills or do things you otherwise would not do.

You may need to convince your boss that you want to – and can handle – taking on more responsibility. You might want to persuade your boss to adjust your work schedule so you can attend a class.

If you want to create more income, you may need to sell your spouse on the idea of you going back to school, or investing some money in starting a part-time business in direct sales or to buy a franchise.

The important point to understand is that selling is a noble and critical component of achieving success. It is as necessary as anything else you will do in your journey.

Accept it, embrace it and learn how to do it well. Read books, take classes, talk to successful people and learn how they have done it. You have to overcome the self-limiting belief that you are not and never want to be a salesperson. The brutal fact: You are a salesperson today, and you will need to be a good one to reach your dream of success. It is an important skill and something that you will always be able to use throughout your life.

Now that we have taken a look at some of the most common self-limiting beliefs, let's get started on identifying the ones affecting you.

CHAPTER 6

Identifying YOUR Self-limiting Beliefs

*"What people say you cannot do,
you try and find that you can."*
– **Henry David Thoreau**

Have you ever had a dream or goal in your life but people kept telling you that it was impossible? That you just could not do what you wanted to do?

Listening to the negative input of others can affect your ability to reach your dreams.

Once upon a time there was a bunch of tiny frogs who arranged a running competition. The goal was to reach the top of a very high tower. A big crowd had gathered around the tower to see the race and cheer on the contestants.

Honestly, no one in the crowd really believed that the tiny frogs would reach the top of the tower. You heard statements such as:

"Oh, WAY too difficult! They will NEVER make it to the top" or "Not a chance that they will succeed. The tower is too high!"

The tiny frogs began collapsing one by one. Except for those who, in a fresh tempo, were climbing higher and higher. The crowd continued to yell, "It is too difficult! No one will make it."

More tiny frogs got tired and gave up. But ONE continued higher and higher and higher. This one wouldn't give up.

At the end, everyone else had given up climbing the tower except for the one tiny frog who, after a big effort, was the only one who reached the top!

Then all of the other tiny frogs naturally wanted to know how this one little frog managed to do it? A contestant asked the tiny frog how he had found the strength to succeed and reach the goal.

It turned out …

The winner was DEAF!!

Never listen to other people's tendencies to be negative or pessimistic. They can take your dreams and goals away from you. Words have a very powerful affect because everything you hear and read will impact your actions. Choose to follow your dream of success and not let others tell you differently.

We all have experiences in life that have established deep-seated beliefs about our abilities and our limits, about what we can do and what we believe we cannot do. Throughout our life, we are held back by these self-limiting beliefs and they shape the lives we live today.

As a result of these beliefs, you might feel uncomfortable doing some of the things you know must be done to achieve your dreams. If you are going to reach success in your life, you must be willing to do things you have never done before in order to get the result you want.

In order to decide what you must do, you need to understand what your self-limiting beliefs are and how to overcome them. The fourth step in conquering your self-limiting beliefs is to identify what is getting in your way and how to deal with it.

One of my favorite movies is *Rudy*. This movie, based on a true story, is a great example of someone who overcame the doubts others had about his ability and accomplished his dream.

All his life, Rudy was told that he just wasn't good enough to play football at Notre Dame. He was too small, too slow and not strong enough. Most of these comments were made by people who loved him. In fact, at one point a teacher wouldn't even let Rudy get on the school's bus that was traveling to Notre Dame for a college visit. This teacher didn't believe that Rudy had what it took to get into the school, let alone play football there.

However, from the time he was a young boy, Rudy lived with the dream of playing football at Notre Dame. He wouldn't let others tell him he couldn't do it.

His blue-collar family laughed at his ambition and told him to be happy settling for a job working in the local steel mill like his father and brother. Rudy wouldn't give up on his dream saying, "My whole life people have been telling me what I could do and couldn't do. I've always listened to them and believed what they said. I don't want to do that anymore." He went to amazing lengths to win admission to Notre Dame and once there, became a walk-on player.

Still no one believed he would ever actually play in a game. His main responsibility on the team was to be little more than a practice dummy for the starting team. But, due to his perseverance and strong beliefs in his dreams, Rudy wins over the hearts of the players. The players actually go to the coaches and demand that Rudy be allowed to play at least one play in the last game of his senior year.

To the amazement of his family, friends and fellow students, Rudy gets a chance to play in the game. The fulfillment of a lifelong dream comes true for Rudy. This is a truly inspirational movie and teaches all of us that we need to listen to our heart and our dreams and not the doubts of others.

Not only have others been telling us all the things we can't do, but we have been telling ourselves what we can't do as well. The major obstacle a person has to doing or having what he wants are his self-limiting beliefs. Many of them are in the subconscious mind and must be identified and changed to positive beliefs in order to remove them as obstacles.

Once you have defined success, created a clear specific vision and set goals to accomplish, you then need to identify what is going to get in your way.

Recognizing a Self-limiting Belief

What are the self-limiting beliefs that are affecting your ability to achieve your dreams in your career, your business and your life's mission? Finding them can be tricky as your mind is very good at hiding them from you. Your mind becomes very content in the comfort zone and it feels safe there. However, the comfort zone can be a bad place to let your mind stay.

When you are in the comfort zone, you are not learning and not growing. In order to grow, you must come out of the comfort zone and try things that you are not accustomed to doing.

In order to identify your Self-limiting beliefs, go back to the goals you wrote in chapter four. Take each one of your goals and say it in the positive present tense. Say specifically that you have what it takes to achieve it.

If you set a goal to start your own business, then say, "I am a very successful business owner." What is your immediate mental response? Does it feel wrong to tell yourself this? Do you think back to yourself, "No, I'm not; I don't have what it takes," or "I don't know how to do that."

If you set a goal to become the highest paid salesperson in your company, say to yourself, "I make more money as a salesperson at my company than any other person there." How does that feel? What is your mental response? If your mind immediately presents you with doubt about your ability to accomplish this, then you have a self-limiting belief that will get in your way.

Self-limiting beliefs cause us to block any conflicting (positive) information while confirming any new negative information. By stating your goals in this way, your hidden assumptions make themselves known. As soon as your self-doubt starts to create resistance, you need to grab hold of it and figure out what is causing it. Where is the self-limiting belief coming from?

> *"I've always believed that you can think positive just as well as you can think negative."*
> – **Sugar Ray Robinson**

More than 90 percent of the people we face everyday are negative. They choose to look at the hole in the middle and not the delicious donut on the outside.

> There was a hunter who came into the possession of a special bird dog. The dog was the only one of its kind, because it could walk on water. One day he invited a friend to go hunting with him so that he could show off his prized bird dog. After some time, they shot a few ducks, which fell into the river. The man ordered his dog to run and fetch the birds from the water. The dog ran on top of the water and grabbed the birds. The man was expecting a compliment about the amazing dog, but did not receive it. Curious, he asked his friend if the friend had noticed anything unusual about the dog. The friend replied, "Yes, I did see something unusual about your dog. Your dog can't swim!"

People are so accustomed to being negative that they will look for the negative and try hard to prove it to themselves before they will accept the positive.

I see this all the time with clients and prospects that I coach. Everyone comes to the coaching program with a series of self-limiting beliefs. I have had very successful business owners who have been unable to accept their success and enjoy it. Others are so used to having the business struggle that, when it starts performing well and creating the profits and freedom they want, they are afraid of the success and instead still look for the negative in the business.

I worked with one business owner who had a great product and excellent opportunities to reach very high levels of success in the business that would support her dreams for her personal life. The problem was, she didn't believe she possessed the ability to take the business to the next level. She had a very strong self-limiting belief that she just didn't have what it takes. She kept looking for the reasons why the business was not getting better.

She made progress in some areas of the business but struggled to do the things she needed to improve in other areas. She stayed focused on the negatives of the business and worked hard to avoid the pain associated with the negatives instead of working hard to move toward the pleasure of success.

Some of her beliefs were in fact valid. At that moment in time, she did not have some of the skills or knowledge she needed. The problem was she believed she would never be able to learn those skills. The difference between a self-limiting belief and a valid recognition of a skill or knowledge deficiency is what you believe.

If you truly believe you will accomplish your goals, your vision and your mission, then you will never doubt your ability to do what you need to do. You will learn to be who you need to be and you will have the things you want in life. You will be able to recognize what you need to learn and what skills you need to develop, but you will not doubt your ability to do it.

Believing that you can and will learn what you need to – and you will do what needs to be done to achieve success – is the difference between a self-limiting belief and a legitimate recognition of what you need to work on to accomplish your goals.

Examining Self-limiting Beliefs

Most of us have looked to outside sources to find the causes of the experiences we have that we don't like. It can be difficult to accept the idea that it's because of our self-limiting beliefs that we are experiencing some of our challenges. However, by finding and changing these beliefs we can gain confidence and overcome them.

Life gives us several forms of feedback on our beliefs. A primary source is through our experiences that have created less than satisfactory results. Many times when we experience negative results we tend to allow them to influence our beliefs about our abilities. This is especially true if the negative result occurs frequently.

In order to find out if a belief is limiting, ask the question, "Does this belief say, *I can't, I don't believe I can* or *Not possible?*" If it does, then your experiences have created a negative belief.

As an example, if you own a business and you have become accustomed to working 70 to 80 hours a week, then you start to develop a belief that you must work this many hours and you are not capable of managing the business in fewer hours. This is one of the many beliefs I see with owners I coach. They have developed a belief that working extended hours is just a part of ownership. They are saying, "I can't work fewer hours and still be successful." Of course, this is not true, but their experience has created this belief over time.

Once a self-limiting belief is identified, ask, "What would someone have to believe to be creating this type of limiting thought?" Write down all the answers that come to mind, including any inner conflicts you have that would lead to this belief. By examining your beliefs in this way, you will begin to identify what you need to remove, learn or change in your life. If you are focused on what you believe you can't do, then your ability to overcome these beliefs will be difficult if not impossible.

"A man is what he thinks about all day long."
– Ralph Waldo Emerson

Change your thinking and you change your world. Once you have created the positive empowering beliefs about your life, then you can apply the rest of what you are learning in this book to create the life you want and accomplish your definition of success.

If you think in positive terms, then you will get a positive result. Self-limiting beliefs will stay limiting unless you believe you can and will change them.

Identify Your Self-limiting Beliefs

To identify the self-limiting beliefs that may get in your way of achieving success, go back to the definition of success you created in Chapter 1. Read your definition in the positive present tense and make note of your immediate mental response. If you have any hesitation or negative thoughts about your belief that this success belongs to you, then write down your reaction on the worksheet at the end of this chapter.

Do the same thing with your vision statements in Chapter 2. Say each one in a positive present tense statement and note your mental reaction. Record those reactions on the worksheet and then proceed to the goals you wrote in Chapter 4 and do the same thing.

You will probably find that some of the same hesitations, negative thoughts or beliefs will come out in all three areas. That is ok and to be expected. If your success definition, vision statements and goals are all in alignment, then you will see consistency in the self-limiting beliefs you identify.

You can overcome all of these self-limiting beliefs once you have identified them and committed to taking positive steps toward changing them. Some of them are simply going to be mental changes you need to make. Think differently about your life, what you can accomplish and who you need to be in order to reach your dreams.

Other self-limiting beliefs will require specific action steps, such as getting more education, improving a specific skill, doing research or finding a mentor to help you along the way.

Whatever you need to allow you to overcome your self-limiting beliefs, now is the time to identify them and make plans to deal with them. Use the following worksheets to document your plan. Be as specific as you possibly can. The more specific you are and the more detail you include, the better you will be able to identify an action plan for overcoming your self-limiting belief.

SELF-LIMITING BELIEF WORKSHEET

Read your definition of success in the positive present tense. What self-limiting beliefs come from your Definition of Success Statement?

_____

_____

_____

_____

_____

_____

_____

Read your vision statements in the positive present tense. What self-limiting beliefs come from your Personal Vision Statements?

_____

_____

_____

_____

_____

_____

_____

Read each of your Personal Goals in the positive present tense. What self-limiting beliefs come from your Goal Statements?

_____

_____

_____

_____

_____

_____

_____

_____

_____

_____

_____

_____

_____

_____

_____

_____

_____

Review all the self-limiting beliefs you have identified above and consolidate any of those that are the same. This will help you narrow the list down to specific beliefs so you can make a plan to eliminate your self-limiting beliefs.

MY ACTION PLAN TO ELIMINATE
MY SELF-LIMITING BELIEFS

Don't be confined by the number of lines provided on the work-sheet. This is simply a guide to help you capture your thoughts. The important thing is to be completely honest with yourself and don't hold back. You will not achieve your success goal if you are not honest about what you need to work on. A realistic self-evaluation is absolutely critical in this exercise.

Self-limiting belief – _____

_____

What information or action do I need to overcome this?

_____

_____

_____

_____

Self-limiting belief – _____

_____

What information or action do I need to overcome this?

_____

_____

_____

_____

Self-limiting belief – _____

_____

What information or action do I need to overcome this?

_____

_____

_____

_____

Self-limiting belief – _____

_____

What information or action do I need to overcome this?

_____

_____

_____

_____

Self-limiting belief – _____

_____

What information or action do I need to overcome this?

_____

_____

_____

_____

CHAPTER 7

The Importance of Strong Mentors

"My chief want in life is someone who shall make me do what I can."
— Ralph Waldo Emerson

When you look back on your life experiences, who were the mentors that helped you learn or grow? Who took you by the hand and gave you encouragement and support, maybe even challenged you at times to do what you didn't want to do? At the beginning of every successful person there was someone who helped him or her along the path toward success.

Mentors have been instrumental in creating some of the most successful men and women in the world. We all have had people like this in our lives and they are absolutely essential to achieving the levels of success you desire.

Now that you have identified your self-limiting beliefs and identified what you need to do to overcome them, it is time to work on how you will do it. The fifth step in conquering your self-limiting beliefs is to identify mentors to support you.

Finding a mentor or mentors to help you along your journey is absolutely essential. You have developed your self-limiting beliefs over many years and thousands of experiences in your life. It is necessary to get someone to support you, guide you and encourage you to do what you need to do and be who you need to be in order to get what you want from life. If you start to fall back into your old ways or get off track, your mentor should push you back on track.

We all need someone to help us accomplish what we truly can in our life. It is so easy to get lost in the day-to-day existence of our life that we start to lose track of what we wanted in the first place. A good mentor will teach you and help you do what you can and should do.

My own mentors helped launch my career and pushed me at times when I needed to move my success to the next level. I achieved the position of Division President of one of the largest banks in the U.S. because someone took an interest in me early in my career and believed in me.

I started my banking career in 1976 at the age of 18, just out of high school and trying to decide what I wanted to do with my life. I had not the slightest idea what my career would be or at that point in life if I was even going to go to college.

Oh, I knew that college was important but my parents couldn't afford to send me to college and I certainly hadn't saved enough money to pay my own way. Student loans were a possibility but why go into all that debt?

I started my career in banking while I decided what to do about college. During my first few years in banking, I was fortunate enough to have someone in the company take an interest in me. I never really understood why, but Henry Steeler, the vice president of human resources for the bank, kept in touch with me and gave me encouraging words. He taught me how to handle myself with senior management.

One day he told me he was recommending me for a new position and took the time to advise me to take the job. It was a teller position and I would get some important experience. He told me to do the job well, show up every day and don't worry about the next position, just do this one to the best of my ability and more opportunities would come.

Henry guided me through several positions. At each step, he took the time to advise me what was important with that job and how that position would help me.

One day, Henry came to me and asked me to represent the Bank on the board of the American Institute of Banking. This is a non-profit industry educational group that offered banking and finance courses to employees of federally insured banks and savings and loans (they still existed back then).

Now, there was no way with my position at the bank that I was qualified to sit on this board, especially since this was a graduating board and in four years I would move up to be president of the board. But Henry believed in me. He gave me the book *Roberts Rule of Orders*, told me how to handle myself in meetings and what I should do when I was in business situations such as a business lunch or dinner, and I was expected to pay. In other words, he mentored me on how to take on a role that I was not qualified for and put me in a position to GROW.

Henry guided me until he retired from the bank. I truly believe that because he took an interest in me and believed in me more than I did, he helped me achieve success faster than I would have on my own.

I was fortunate that someone took an early interest in me and taught me the importance of mentors. Throughout my career, I have looked for my next mentor and made it my point to help mentor others.

Exercise

Take a few minutes and think back on the mentors you have had in your life. It might be someone that inspired you in school, maybe a teacher or family member. Maybe it was someone that helped you get started in your career or took an interest in you when you were trying to make an important decision in your life.

Create a list of people that have inspired or coached you and how they helped you. This will help you to start thinking about what qualities you will look for in the mentors you choose as you move forward in your success journey.

Mentor: _____

What they helped me achieve: _____

_____

What qualities did they exhibit: _____

_____

Mentor: _____

What they helped me achieve: _____

_____

What qualities did they exhibit: _____

_____

Continue to list as many mentors as you can remember. The more you can identify, the better you will be able to recognize what traits they brought to the table that were important to you. If you are not able to come up with any mentors that have helped you so far, don't worry. You will be able to find a mentor to help you move forward using the information provided in this chapter.

Why Do I Need a Mentor – I Can Do This on My Own

When Tiger Woods became a professional golfer in 1996, he took the golfing world by storm. He immediately began chasing the record books winning the 1997 Masters tournament in his first attempt as a pro in the Masters.

In 2003, Tiger was considered to be at the top of his game, but still he knew he could be better. He hired Hank Haney to be his swing coach and went to work on improving an already amazing golf game. Tiger received a lot of criticism for this decision and went into a slump in golf's major tournaments. In fact, he played in ten major championships without a victory.

Tiger and Hank continued to work diligently on making the changes Tiger wanted to make. In 1995, he won the Masters tournament at Augusta National and began a run that has been unprecedented in golf.

Tiger, an amazing talent, saw the value in working with a coach to help him achieve even higher levels of success. If someone as talented as Tiger Woods understands the importance of having a coach working with him to reach his goals, then certainly all of us can find value in working with a mentor.

So often I hear people say they don't need any help. It is so hard for some people to ask for help or to admit that having someone to guide them would be valuable. Many fear that asking for help might be seen as a sign of weakness.

Our environment is a major factor in creating this mind-set. In the work place, you are taught that you are in competition with everyone there. If you want a promotion or to garner the favor of the boss, you need to perform better than everyone else does.

If you want to get ahead, you need to compete. When you ask for help, you find out that others maybe aren't so willing to offer it because it may give you an edge over them. You begin to understand this and take on the same mentality. You learn to keep things to yourself so that others won't get ahead of you.

When you need to improve a skill or improve your performance, you figure out you must do it yourself. Then after all your hard work, you finally earn your promotion. Once you have achieved the promotion, you must figure out how to do your new job.

Most people will not go to their new boss and tell them they are not sure exactly how to do some of their new responsibilities out of fear. Maybe the boss will think you weren't ready for the promotion and start to doubt you.

Instead, you believe it is up to you to figure it out all alone. You learn that if you want to succeed in the corporate world asking for help is a sign of weakness not strength.

The same is true if you start your own business. When you go out on your own, there will be people who will doubt your ability to succeed. You may even have some doubts yourself.

In order to prove everyone wrong, you feel the need to figure it out without asking for help. The thought enters your mind that if you ask for help then people will figure out you don't know it all. Heaven forbid that you might not have all the answers yourself.

The truth is, asking for support and guidance from a trusted mentor and advisor is a sign of strength.

Nobody has all the answers. A willingness to ask for help and accept the wisdom and support of a mentor means you are ready to open yourself up to new learning and challenges. It is a sign of trust and confidence to seek the counsel of others. To achieve your definition of success and remove self-limiting beliefs from your life, it is absolutely necessary that you continually learn and grow.

Finding Your Mentor

How do you go about finding the right mentor for you? There may be many mentors along your journey depending on where you are in the process. Think about your needs and what you'd like your mentor to do for you. It's important to consider the type of support you want your mentor to provide. There will be different personal and professional needs, but a good mentor can help you through both.

To choose a good mentor, you need to ask yourself uncomfortable questions. What are my weaknesses? Am I prepared to be challenged? Am I prepared to be pushed out of my comfort zone and to accept the 'tough love' of a mentor? Ideally you want people that will inspire you and demonstrate the skills, attributes and attitudes you would like to exhibit.

You may need your mentor to push you to challenge yourself more than you might otherwise push yourself. They may also need to give you ideas about where to get the help you need to learn new skills or for continuing education. You will also want them to listen to you as well as to offer advice.

Think about your personality style and what type of person will complement and benefit you best. Consider talking to others about their mentors and any recommendations they have.

Then consider possible mentors that may be available. It's important to consider all the possibilities when it comes to finding a mentor. A professional coach trained in the art of mentoring and personal and/or business development can help you. When hiring a professional coach, look for someone that matches your needs.

Keep an open mind in matching your needs to a prospective mentor. He or she may be able to help you in ways you hadn't planned. Your circle of friends, colleagues, bosses and family offer a good starting point in your search. You can also expand your search to include teachers, business leaders, spiritual or religious leaders or other significant people in your life.

The mentor you choose will depend on what your personal life plan is and the type of self-limiting beliefs you have. Take a hard look at the self-limiting beliefs you identified in the last chapter when looking at possible mentors and make sure the person(s) you choose will be able to help you address these areas.

Think about how you want to approach and ask someone to mentor you. Understand that some mentors will charge a fee to provide you with their service. Others will be happy to mentor you for free. The decision as to which is right for you depends on what you need to achieve and how much you feel you need the expertise of a professional.

Do not assume that just because someone will agree to mentor you for free that is the right path for you. If you need support starting, growing a business, moving quickly to develop new skills for a promotion or making major changes in your life, then a professional may be the best choice.

Whichever path you decide is right for you, the most important point is to make sure the person and their skills and knowledge of how to be a mentor are appropriate for you.

What to Look For in a Mentor

When deciding on a mentor, you should consider the following list of attributes.

A mentor should:

- provide you with support and encouragement
- be willing to hold you accountable to taking the action you need to take to accomplish your goals
- help you to learn from your mistakes and failures
- be connected to resources that will help you move closer to your goal
- provide support and training in areas important to your success
- be a friend, but not nice enough to let you off the hook when you aren't moving forward
- help you identify your strengths and weaknesses and recommend how to use them or improve them as needed
- take an interest in the achievement of your success
- be a good listener and ask tough questions
- challenge you to improve and take risks

- lift you up when you are feeling discouraged
- demonstrate personal and professional integrity

A good mentor must be genuine in their desire to help you and take a real interest in seeing you succeed.

I have worked with and talked to coaches and business leaders from all over the world. If there is one trait I find common in all the successful ones, it is the passion, dedication and desire to see their mentee succeed. Whoever you choose for your mentoring relationship, make sure they bring this same level of commitment and dedication to your success.

Interview prospective mentors and explain what your goals are and what you feel you need help achieving. Again, you can hire a coach; ask a business leader, a peer, friend or family member. Just make sure that whoever becomes your mentor has the time, skills, devotion and willingness to help you and be there on a regular basis to give you guidance and feedback.

Making the Relationship Work for You

Once you have decided on a mentor and they have agreed to help you, how will you make the relationship work? Is it as simple as getting someone to agree to it? Unfortunately, it may not be that simple.

In order for the relationship to be of value to you in achieving the success you are aiming for, you must be willing to work at it. Your mentor needs to be willing and able to hold you account-able to do what you say you are going to do. Having a mentor who lets you get away with not completing the steps required to achieve your goals will only hurt your ability to get where you want to go.

It is also important that the mentor is available to you by phone or in person on a regular basis. Having regular contact will keep you moving forward and give you the motivation to do what you need to do before your next meeting. We tend to be more productive when we have a deadline to meet or have made a commitment to someone and don't want to tell them you didn't get "it" done.

You must also be willing to accept there will be days when you may not like your mentor. If your mentor is willing to push you and call you out when you fall behind or start to complain, then there will be days when you will get a little upset with them.

It is their job to push you and be honest with you. It is your job to accept it and learn from it. You will need to work through the pressure and stress that can sometimes come from taking on the challenges you need to do to reach your goals. A good mentor will care enough about your success to confront you when you need it and reward you when you make progress.

You also must be willing to share your success definition, personal vision statement, SMART goals and your self-limiting beliefs with your mentor.

> **If you are not willing to honestly share this level of detail and intimacy with your mentor, then you have chosen the wrong person. Confidence and trust are critical in this relationship.**

Summary

Choosing a mentor you can work with and who will keep you focused on your dreams is very important to help you overcome your self-limiting beliefs and reach success. Take the self-limiting beliefs you identified and share them with your mentor. Make sure you also share the plan you put in place to overcome these beliefs. Sharing your dreams and goals with someone else makes your dreams become very real and raises your commitment to pursuing them.

Your mentor will help you work through the plan and let you know if you start to slip into old habits or if your self-limiting belief starts to get in the way of what you are trying to accomplish. It will be much easier for your mentor to identify a self-limiting belief that is starting to get in your way then it will be for you to do on your own.

You will be better prepared to face the challenges you will encounter if you have someone to encourage you, push you and reward you along the way. Hire a coach or find a trusted advisor that will not be nice enough to let you get away with not taking action.

Choose wisely and you will be amazed at how fast you will start making progress toward your dreams. Don't underestimate the importance of this critical step in achieving the life you want. Sharing your dreams with someone else is a very powerful motivator and a good mentor will be invaluable in your journey. Once you have chosen a mentor and reached an agreement about how you will work together, it is time to get started working together to build the life you desire.

"I never cease to be amazed at the power of the coaching process to draw out the skills or talent that was previously hidden within an individual, and which invariably finds a way to solve a problem previously thought unsolvable."

– John Russell, Managing Director
Harley-Davidson Europe Ltd.

CHAPTER 8

Success Comes From Lifelong Learning

"Man's mind, once stretched by a new idea, never regains its original dimensions."
– Oliver Wendell Holmes

When you graduated from high school or college, did you have a big graduation party? You thought your education was behind you and now it was time to go out and get a job, make some money and start working your way up the corporate ladder or start your own business.

After so many years in school, you were happy to be free of the classroom and the studying. There was probably some sadness about the good times you had with your friends and classmates coming to an end. It is with some trepidation that you moved into the working world and its responsibilities.

When I graduated from high school, I wasn't able to afford college and knew that I had to get a job. I was looking forward to getting out into the working world and starting to earn some money. College was important but making money sounded good too.

While I was looking for a job, I decided to apply at the local brick manufacturing company. I needed somewhere to work right away and, while I knew I didn't want to make bricks for a career, I knew it paid well and I thought I could get a job pretty quickly.

When I went to see the supervisor to apply, he told me there was a long waiting list of people that had applied ahead of me. He gave me a short interview, more as a courtesy than anything else. However, at the end of the interview, I looked him right in the eye, shook his hand and with all the confidence I could muster said, "I know you have a lot of people on that list, but if you want an employee that will show up every day, work hard and give you an honest 100 percent effort every day, then I'm the employee you want."

I received a call two days later offering me that job. I was amazed but learned a valuable lesson that day. I learned very quickly the importance of asking for what you want, showing confidence and taking action. I also learned that I would always be learning. Life is full of lessons if we just stop and pay attention.

Success is a journey and will take time and effort, as well as a strong positive mental attitude. You will need to learn many new things along the journey. Success requires lifelong learning in a variety of ways. In order to remove the self-limiting beliefs you have identified, it will require you to take steps to constantly learn and accept new ideas, new skills and new knowledge.

Learning can come in many ways and through many sources. I learned an important lesson at the age of 18 about not being afraid to ask for what you want, just by taking a chance on a job interview. I quickly learned making bricks was not for me, and I lasted a very short time. Fortunately, my job opportunity at the bank came quickly and I started my new career in banking!

Why Continual Learning Is Critical

Your personal comfort zone can be a very bad place to stay. Staying in the comfort zone means you are doing things you are used to, the way you are used to doing them. When you are in the comfort zone, you are not learning.

How to Boil a Bullfrog is a story that illustrates comfort zones very well.

> Years ago, scientists did a simple experiment on a bullfrog. They threw a bullfrog into a container of boiling water, and the bullfrog instantly popped out of the boiling water. Next, they put the bullfrog into a container of cold water. The bullfrog liked it, stayed in the container and was very happy and content. The scientists then turned on the heat at the bottom of the container. As the water got warmer, the bullfrog relaxed and took a nap. The bullfrog was so comfortable that it just stayed in the container and was "cooked."

Most of us like staying in the comfort zone. We have a house to go home to, a comfortable bed to sleep in, family, friends and a job, even though we may or may not really like it. But, it is comfortable. We have worked hard to get where we are today and don't like to rock the boat.

In reality, most of us are like the bullfrog. We are comfortable, if not completely happy, and don't want to see our comfort zone shook up. In life and in our career, if we are not learning, we are not growing. The world around us is constantly changing and moving at an amazing pace. Keeping up is one thing, but doing the things you need to do to move ahead is another altogether.

There is no such thing as "staying where we are," because there is always something new to learn. If you are going to achieve your definition of success in life, then you will always need to be learning something new.

If you truly believe in the vision you have for your life and are willing to take the action needed to achieve that vision, then continuing to grow and learn is critical. There are opportunities to learn and grow all around you every day.

In order to take advantage of these learning opportunities, you must open your mind to them and place the needs you have into your Reticular Activating System. By identifying what you need to learn and making yourself open to it, you will find the opportunities coming available to you.

Sources for Continued Learning

"The only difference between where you are now and where you'll be next year are the books you read and the people you meet."
– **Charlie Jones**

Granted, some of your learning may need to be classroom or program based but some of it will come from your mentor or other people. Every 90 days, when you write your 90-day objectives, you will want to identify what learning you need and where it will come from.

Once you have identified what you need to learn, the next step is to determine what books to read, who to talk to, what class to take, or what other source you need to reference. Let's take a look at some of the more common sources of learning available to you.

Reading

A lot of your learning will come from your day-to-day experiences, what you read and whom you meet.

> *"The man who doesn't read good books has no advantage over the man who can't read them."*
> **– Mark Twain**

Reading is a great source of expanding your mind and gathering knowledge. There are so many great books available to read on just about any subject. At the end of this book, there is a suggested reading list of books.

A requirement for my clients is to learn through reading. I assign clients books to read on subjects we are working on or things they need to learn in their business. You can get so many different perspectives through books.

There are also magazines and trade journals for just about all aspects of business and life. A simple internet search will give you a list of publications suited to your area of interest.

The great part is that you don't have to agree with everything you read. What is important is, by reading, you open your mind to other ways of thinking about things. By challenging your mind with new ideas, even if you disagree with them, it causes you to think differently. It may even cause confusion as you absorb what you read.

Confusion is a good thing though. When you are confused, it causes you to think through the issue and maybe even study it some. By doing this, you are learning and growing. Confusion gets you out of the comfort zone.

Be a sponge for new knowledge and learn from the experts through their books, magazines, newsletters and periodicals. I have a goal to read two business or self-help books a month. I also subscribe to three business magazines and receive numerous on-line newsletters from experts on many subjects. If I can pick up even one or two new ideas from each of these sources, I know my business will continue to be successful, I will continue to grow as a person and I will be better able to contribute to the success of others. It's truly amazing how much help is out there when you start looking.

Social Networking

Seeking out and asking others for help is referred to as networking. Today there is more than one way to network. The advent of social networking sites offers a completely new avenue of opportunity.

Basically, social networking is a way that people of similar interests connect. The beauty is that this happens when people you may not know find you because of some connection they have with someone you both know.

Now you can talk to, get advice from and learn from people all over the world 24 hours a day, seven days a week. Social networking internet sites are popping up all the time. Sites like *YouTube, Facebook* and *MySpace* are million-member general networking sites. You may need sites more specific to your interest or needs, so sites like *LinkedIn, XING*, and *Ecademy* focus on business networking while *43 Things* focuses on goals and dreams networking. A quick internet search will yield a list of sites and their focus so you can choose the one right for you.

Certainly a lot of what is available on these sites is not going to help you in your journey. Watching someone make funny faces, juggle or break dance is probably not what you need to get ahead. However, finding the right sites will offer areas where you can have a meaningful dialogue with one person or a group of people about subjects helpful to your goals.

Another option is to create your own social networking forum to exchange ideas and get support. As I started writing this book, I became aware of several sites I could participate in to help support me in the writing and promotion of my book. The Book Marketing Network social networking site is specifically for authors and publishers to network and support each other. From this site, you can also set up your own social network group.

The possibilities are endless in the internet age. Determine what areas you are seeking support in or what you need to get advice on and do a little research. You will be amazed at how much help you will get. Just don't be afraid to ask and you'll get support.

Traditional Networking

Another source for learning is your mentor. Other people you meet will also present a constant source of learning. Every day you will meet people you can learn from. Observe others and you will learn what works, what to do and what not to do.

While this passive learning is good, what you really must do is make a concerted effort to learn from others. Seek out those that can help you along your journey.

Develop your "A-Team" of people you can talk to and network with. These are the people you know who have knowledge in the area where you are trying to make contacts and gain skills or expertise.

They may work for your company or be connected in the community. Your Chamber of Commerce can be a good source of contacts as well as local centers of influence such as attorney's, CPA's, church leaders or your circle of friends.

Don't be afraid to call someone in your area of interest and ask them to meet with you. You will find that many people will be willing to help and be flattered that you asked. Successful people like to feel like they belong to something bigger than just themselves. You want to associate with and learn from successful people so that is who you should be calling.

Some of the most successful people I know are the ones who have a wide network. When I was first starting out in the banking business, I was working hard to get ahead and learn as much as I could. My father-in-law, Dr. William Babeaux, really understood the concept of having a strong network. He was involved in many different areas of business including having his own Orthodontic practice and working for the State in different capacities within the public health system.

He had a wide network of contacts and – in order to help me in my career – he offered to set up some lunch meetings so I could meet influential people in the financial industry that he knew. I remember attending one of these lunches at an exclusive private dining club. It was one of those places with the big leather chairs, artwork on the walls and cigar smoke hanging in the air. At 25 years old, I was a little intimidated by the whole thing.

The man we met with was the CEO of one of the local banks. Not only was my father-in-law kind enough to give his time to do this for me but, this CEO of a local bank was willing to give some of his valuable time to meet with me and give me advice.

After a few of these kinds of meetings, I began to understand how important it was to have a strong network and to work it. This also taught me that people at all levels will help if you ask them and are sincere in your desire to listen and learn something from them. They will take an interest in your success, and you will even find that some of them will go way out of their way to help you.

Behind every successful person is a large strong network, one that has been built and nurtured over time.

You need to be willing and able to participate in the network of others to help them in return. By giving back to your network, you will create strong relationships, and they will open many doors of opportunity for you. This give and take approach will teach you so much and be invaluable.

Continuing Education Classes/Programs

When was the last time you took a look at the educational opportunities available in your community? Did you realize there is an almost endless source of educational classes, seminars, workshops and presentations everywhere? You don't have to sign up for a college diploma program to get some classroom education.

I am constantly amazed at how many times I find myself back in one education program or another. After earning my bachelor's degree, I went to banking school and earned a degree from the American Bankers Association School of Retail Banking. Then I went into a Master's Degree program. Next thing I knew, I was in an intense training program to earn a certification as a business coach.

During all that time, I was constantly attending workshops, speeches, corporate training programs and the list just goes on. It didn't take me long to realize that the learning process never ends. There are so many great programs available that it is sometimes hard to choose.

Look in your local paper for speeches or seminars being held in your area. There are so many inspirational speakers who offer insights from their life experiences that can be extremely valuable. Recently our town had Christopher Gardner visit and talk about his remarkable experience.

Mr. Gardner is the man behind the story *The Pursuit of Happiness;* The story of a man who had to re-make his life when an unfortunate set of circumstances forced him from his job and home. He went on to achieve an amazing level of success and became an inspiration to millions.

Hearing people like Mr. Gardner talk about their story and how they persevered is very powerful and really helps motivate you to action. There are many speakers out there that can do the same for you.

You will also find free or low cost seminars offered. If you want to learn more about money management, go to a seminar put on by a local financial advisor. If you want to learn about business or selling, then check with your local chamber of commerce or look in the business section of the paper for seminars being offered. These type of programs are offered frequently; all you need to do is commit the time and go.

In my coaching business, we offer free or low cost seminars and workshops all the time. I am constantly amazed at how many people don't take advantage of them. I believe that many times people do not attend these programs because they fear (there's that word again!) being sold something. This is absurd. You can attend, learn and grow your skills at these programs; if someone gives you a brief sales pitch, you just don't have to buy. You will still learn a great deal. You don't have to buy, but you may find that what is being offered is of great value to you.

If you attend a seminar put on by a local financial advisor, you will learn some important information about financial planning, but you may also find the advisor can help you achieve your goals. Why not listen and then decide instead of deciding before you even go? You miss learning important information just to avoid possibly needing to say no to a sales pitch. Eliminate this fear from your thinking.

Of course, you can also attend courses at the local community college. There are many adult education programs available. If you need to improve your writing, financial literacy, accounting, public speaking, computer skills, small business, management, leadership or just about any technical skill, you will find a class to help you.

There are also classes available through many high schools, libraries, community groups and city services. The point is there are all kinds of opportunities available to you; all you have to do is spend some time looking for them.

Don't let any of the excuses you may have used in the past get in the way. Eliminate them and don't give yourself any excuse not to do what you know you must in order to stay on the path toward success. Time and money cannot get in your way. You may need to adjust your spending for a short time period to invest in your future. By choosing programs that help you move closer to success, you will find the money spent is a very wise investment.

I have a friend who really wants to leave his current job in banking and become a college professor teaching history. He has a wife and two children, a mortgage and all the responsibilities that come with this type of life. He is very family oriented and a truly great person.

Even though he knows what he wants to do, there is a lot of fear associated with making this type of change. Where will he find the time and money to go back to school? Even if he does get the necessary advanced degree, how will he find a job, and will he be able to support his family on the new salary?

These are all valid concerns, but they can't stop him from taking the steps to achieve this goal. He knows in his heart this is what he wants, and his family would support him in his pursuit of it. He knows he needs to go back to school, and now it's time for him to find a way to do it. It's all about taking the first step and realizing that – every day – he needs to just take one more step, and he will get where he wants to go.

The same is true for you. If you need to take classes, attend workshops or other programs, then just do it. Figure out what it will take and make it happen. Going back to school or attending programs does not have to be intimidating. Don't let your fears about it hold you back.

> *"If you will spend an extra hour each day of study in your chosen field, you will be a national expert in that field in five years or less."*
> **– Earl Nightingale**

On-line Research

The internet has made conducting research a much easier proposition these days. You can research and find information on just about any subject. Of course, there is also a lot of misinformation, but there is also an amazing amount of legitimate information for you to use.

If you need to conduct some research to learn about a particular career or industry, you will find it on the internet. There are also many on-line schools that offer a lot of flexibility.

Don't overlook the internet as a source of information to help you improve in your current career as well. If you are in sales and you need to improve your sales skills or your income, use the internet to learn information about your target customer and their company before making the sales call. Join some sales blogs and get ideas from other successful sales professionals. You can sign-up for sales newsletters to learn from sales experts. You can also locate on-line e-books about sales. There are many different things you can do to learn how to become a great salesperson.

This is just one example of how you can use the internet to help you professionally. The same holds true regarding your personal goals. You will be able to find information and contacts on these goals as well. Regardless of what you are trying to accomplish in your goals you can find the resources to help. If you are looking to change careers or industries or start your own business, there is an abundant amount of information at your fingertips.

Work to Learn

Another very effective way to improve your skills and learn important life lessons is to work in your field of interest. For example, if your passion is to open your own donut shop and you don't know anything about making donuts or running a donut shop, then take a job working for someone you respect in a do-nut shop and ask to be put on every possible job there is. Learn how to prepare the dough, how to cook the donuts, how to create the fillings, how to run the register, how to open and close and run the inventory system. Learn it all and don't worry about the money.

Once you have learned all you can, then move on to the next step of your journey to open a donut shop. Keep moving forward until you have everything you need to open your own shop and then do it. The knowledge you will get from working beside someone who is knowledgeable and successful is invaluable. This is real life experience, and you can't get it anywhere else.

If you want to learn how to run a business, find out all the pieces and then take different jobs, internships or volunteer your time in companies or associations where you can learn. Find somewhere to learn accounting and financial management; somewhere to learn sales and marketing. Maybe find another place to learn how to manage people and another to understand inventory control. No matter what you need to learn, you can find somewhere to work or volunteer to get that knowledge.

In fact, you may need to do some things you really are not interested in but need to learn. Many of the clients I work with do not like the accounting and financial management required to run their business. They still need to know it. Many of them didn't learn this lesson until they had already started the business and it became critical for them. Determine what you need to learn to achieve your goal and learn it even if it is not something you like. It will help you in the long run to be much more successful.

Remember Willie King who volunteered his time working in a shop just so he could learn how to fix transmissions? Willie did this because he knew doing so would allow him to someday own his own business. Willie was a very smart man and has now turned his dream into a reality.

"Learn to earn" is a phrase I use in my coaching practice to signify how important it is to continue to learn if you want to earn in life.

Learn to earn the success you want in life as well as the wealth you desire.

Your circumstances may make it difficult for you to work full-time for free or at a much lower income than you earn today. Don't let that stop you. Just working a few hours a week or on the weekends will allow you to gain the knowledge and skills you need while still supporting your current life. If you truly desire to achieve your definition of success and create the vision you have for your life, it may be necessary for you to put in some extra time for a while.

While your friends and co-workers are watching re-runs over and over again, you will be putting in time learning and growing and getting ever closer to achieving your success. Then you will live the life you long for, and they will still be complaining about why their life and job aren't what they thought it would be.

The Most Important Lesson of All

At the 2005 Indianapolis 500 motor race, a relatively unknown driver Danica Patrick got her name emblazoned on the front page of the sports section all over the country. She had managed to become the first female driver ever to lead the coveted race with only a few laps to go. It was a true underdog story with a tiny 100-pound woman racing against the men of the Indy Racing

League. Danica is a fierce competitor, and she saw that race as just another chance to race her best and win.

Danica is a quick learner and although she made two rookie mistakes that almost put her out of contention for the title, she still almost managed to win. One of her rookie errors was stalling her car on a mid-race pit stop. This mistake put her at the back of the pack. However, her determination to overcome her mistake led her through the pack and up to 8th place where she made a pit stop on a caution flag and restarted the race.

During the restart, tragedy struck again as she made the mistake of hitting another car with her front wing causing her to limp back into the pits missing half of her front wing. The pit crew replaced the front wing, but the mistake forced her to take an extra long pit stop that put her down a lap. Although she was mad at herself for making these mistakes, she was also determined to learn from them.

She realized being down a lap was something she was going to have to deal with. Her team decided she would stay out on the track when everyone else pitted. In mere seconds, she went from a lap down to leading the race. The big question was whether her fuel and tires would last to the end of the race? Danica was now doing something no other woman had ever done – leading the Indy 500!

While the world watched, she took on the best of the field in racing. With only a few laps to go, her car started to run out of gas. Her car ran out of gas on the final turn and she ended up in fourth place but she had still managed to place higher than any woman in history in this prestigious race. Danica had managed to overcome her mistakes and take her place in history. You can feel confident that Danica learned a lot that day that will help her achieve even greater things in the future.

Learning from all our life lessons and mistakes is the most important lesson of all. Why? Because the life lessons of experience is the best teacher of all. We need to recognize a lesson when it happens so we can use it to help us grow.

**Never say, "Oops." Always say,
"Ah, isn't that interesting."**

Mistakes are wonderful lessons. There is barely a day that goes by when we don't make some type of mistake or where life doesn't try to teach us a lesson. The problem is we tend to get angry about our mistakes or pretend they didn't happen. We might even try to explain them away or find someone or something else to blame for the mistake.

This is the wrong thing to do. You should embrace your mistakes and be honest with yourself. Ask yourself the question, "What happened and why did it happen? What could I have done to change the outcome, and what do I need to do now?" Then ask yourself, "What did I learn from this to help me the next time?" Honest answers are powerful tools that help you grow.

*"The only real mistake is the one from
which we learn nothing."*
– **John Powell**

Exercise

Now that you understand the importance of continual learning, go back and look at your definition of success, your vision statement and your goals, and decide what additional learning you need to do. You will have identified some of the key areas of learning as a part of the exercises you have already done so far.

Take some time now and decide if there is any area you need to identify and what resources are available to you.

Are there any jobs or positions in your company you should work in to learn skills you will require? Are there any skills you can improve through a workshop, seminar or class? What about networking groups to make contacts in your community or industry? Do you need to get involved in a social networking group to get support toward your goal? List your learning needs in the space provided below. Then make sure these are identified in your goals and built into your 90-day objectives.

Key learning needs:

1) _____

2) _____

3) _____

4) _____

5) _____

Summary

You must constantly be learning if you want to achieve the success you desire. Learn to earn is the key message you should take away from this chapter. It is about earning wealth as well as about achieving success in your career, business, relationships, hobbies and all areas of your life.

Learning occurs every day and some of it will come from the mistakes you make and the lessons life sends your way. A good resource for information is through networking and participation in classes, programs and activities. Don't be afraid to take on jobs you are not really excited about, or work for free or in community groups to learn skills you will need.

If your vision of success is to own a business, there will likely be areas you need to learn by attending classes, workshops, seminars or taking on jobs where you can learn those skills. Consult your mentor, network or a coach about what skills you need to know and how to go about acquiring them.

To achieve success, you need to eliminate any self-limiting beliefs you have about doing what it takes to learn what you need. Accept learning as a way of life and become a sponge for new knowledge.

> *"All of the top achievers I know are life-long learners ... looking for new skills, insight, and ideas. If they're not learning, they're not growing ... not moving toward excellence."*
> **– Denis Waitley**

CHAPTER 9

Breaking Through the Barriers to Change

"If you don't change your beliefs, your life will be like this forever. Is that good news?"
– Douglas Noel Adams

Have you ever been so dissatisfied with something going on in your life and became so fed up you decided to change it? You said, "That's it, I'm not doing this anymore." Then you set about making a change. Maybe it was your job. You stopped enjoying the work, or the boss – and decided it was time to find a new job. The dissatisfaction was so intense that you just could not stand it anymore. It may have been something to do with a relationship or your weight or any number of things. Whatever it was, you finally decided to do something about it.

All of us have been in this situation before. It took a lot for us to make a significant change in our life. Why is it so hard for us to make changes? Staying in your comfort zone, is dangerous. Remember, when you stay in your comfort zone you are not learning and not growing. The same is true about change. If you stay in your comfort zone doing the same things you have always done, you will not grow and move closer to your goals.

It is so easy to want to keep doing what you know how to do; what is comfortable and offers no risk. The issue though is that in order to follow the path to success and do all the things you have identified so far, you must change.

> **You must be willing to do what you have not done before if you expect to get different results than you are getting now.**

Ask yourself, "Is it good news if your life stays as it is today … forever?" I am guessing that it isn't if you are reading this book. You have made a decision that you want more from life and you are willing to do what it takes to get that life.

Sometimes change isn't easy, but many times it is easier than we believe it will be. Many times what we fear might happen by making change is far worse than the reality we will experience once the change occurs. We fear the unknown and the uncertainty the change will bring about; however, most of the time what we fear does not actually ever come about.

Think back on a time in your life when you made a big change in your life. Before you made the change, you probably had a lot of "what if" thoughts like, "what if I don't like it" or "what if others think I'm crazy to do this." Once you made the change, you probably discovered that most —if not all – of the "what if's" you thought up never even happened.

Attitude Is the First Step

"The most significant change in a person's life is a change of attitude. Right attitudes produce right actions."
– **William J. Johnston**

Before you can expect any meaningful change to occur, you may need to evaluate your attitude regarding change. Not long ago I was talking to a prospect who owns a plastics company. He was considering starting a coaching program and we were talking about what his concerns were for his business. We also reviewed what changes he felt were required to turn the company into the business he wanted.

He discussed what he felt he needed to do and really seemed to understand that it was important for him to change his beliefs and his actions to get the results he wanted. He realized his office staff was managing him, and he had lost control of the office team. He had been enabling them to get away with doing what they wanted at the pace they wanted and not according to the standards he expected. It was also important to change the systems he had in place for production and inventory control. The systems currently in place were creating workflow issues and delivery problems. He would have to change the way the process was managed and the processes used to handle inventory and finished products that were ready to ship.

But, when we started to talk about what it would take to make those changes and how he personally would have to change, he started to back off. He admitted it would be very hard for him to change. His fear of change started to overcome his desire to achieve his goals. I could see it in his face and read it in his body language. This was going to be a challenge for him.

This situation is not unusual. I see this happen in so many business owners and professionals I talk to and coach. Realizing they need to make changes and actually executing the actions necessary to make the changes are two completely different things. Too many people will rationalize leaving things the way they are to avoid making changes that might create uncertainty or discomfort.

> *"Faced with the choice between changing one's*
> *mind and proving that there is no need to do so,*
> *almost everyone gets busy on the proof."*
> **– John Kenneth Galbraith**

In order to prepare for change, you need to create an attitude of change. You must open your mind and broaden your view of how change will improve your situation and move you closer to achieving success. Accepting that change is a good thing will allow you to remove some of the fear associated with these changes. The good news is that your attitude is in your control. You get to chose what attitude you bring to the change process.

Remove any negativity from your thinking and approach change with a belief that the change will have a positive impact on your success journey. Wake up every day and tell yourself how thankful you are for the opportunity to take the steps necessary to accomplish success in your life, including making changes in your life. Keeping a positive attitude and recognizing the changes are helpful to you will make it much easier to embrace change.

Overcoming Fear Is the Next Step

Most of the things you fear about change are simply in your mind and not real. How many times have you been unhappy about making a change and then, after the process was over, you looked back and decided it wasn't nearly as bad as you thought? Work processes are a prime example.

About 25 years ago, the banking industry went through a major change. The industry was deregulated and the result was banking became much more competitive. No longer could the bankers sit at their desk and wait for customers to come to them. Banks were suddenly competing on interest rates for savings and loan products. New products were introduced that created more competitive marketing.

Bankers began to realize that, in order to compete, they needed to become salespeople. Imagine that, bankers needing to sell. Branch employees were shocked at the idea they had to become salespeople. That meant learning new skills, asking people to buy their products and making sales calls. A lot of branch employees quit instead of trying to change. They just couldn't fathom the idea they had to become a salesperson. This scared them and, in many cases, they were offended they would have to sell. They became bankers so they wouldn't have to be a salesperson.

Many banks started to make the shift quickly, but some bank executives were in denial and wouldn't change. Many of the banks in denial didn't last very long and were acquired by other banks that were faster to react to the changes in the market. The fear of change ran through all levels of the bank and it took many years for the culture to change. Many banks had to replace 50 percent or more of their branch employees before they started to see any major changes.

I was amazed by the resistance to change I encountered at every bank where I worked. The fear employees had about learning how to sell was huge. The fear they felt was totally irrational. Selling bank products was not hard or scary, and there was no reason to resist this change. Granted, not everyone wants to sell. Some of the employees quit because they wanted to change careers and that was fine. But, many of them were fired because they chose to resist the change and failed. Their fear was unfounded and lead to unnecessary grief.

Don't resist change because of fear. If a change is occurring and you aren't sure how you are going to react to it, give it a chance to work for you. The best thing you can do is embrace the change and give it a chance to work.

While some changes are forced on you, like those in the banking industry, most of the changes you are going to make on your journey to success will be your own doing. Apply this same principle to the changes you are going to create in your own life by embracing them and being thankful for the opportunity to learn from them.

Maintain positive motivation and momentum as you make the changes you identify. By staying positive, focused and forward looking you will be able to keep your fear in check and overcome it. Being motivated is a powerful tool in keeping you moving in the right direction and not getting derailed. Fear will not control your actions if you stay focused on what is your end goal.

Identify Areas of Dissatisfaction

What caused you to pick up this book and start reading? Was there some area of your life that you were dissatisfied with and wanted to improve? Did you realize that, in order to achieve the unlimited success you want in life, you will need to do some things differently than you have in the past? Those are the things you need to identify now.

What is it you are dissatisfied with, or what is keeping you from achieving success? What is holding you back? Do you need to change to make you feel happy with you and your ability to achieve your dreams? Take stock of all areas of your life. If you are unhappy with your weight, relationships, current job, business results, commute time, exercise habits, money management or other areas of your life, then you will be very challenged to overcome your self-limiting beliefs and achieve success.

Decide what you need to fix and create your list of things you will no longer tolerate in your life. Start with the heading, "I will no longer tolerate … ." Examples may be;

"I will no longer tolerate …"

- being 20 pounds overweight
- feeling poorly because I do not exercise
- driving 45 minutes to work each day
- working 60+ hours a week
- having an unprofitable business
- not understanding how I spend my money
- not saving any money to help me reach my goals
- running up credit card debt
- going to work everyday and dreading it

Make your list of all the things you are dissatisfied with and will no longer tolerate. Be specific and be honest. This is your life and – if you are really going to make the changes necessary – you need to be honest with yourself. If you can't be honest with yourself, then you certainly won't be able to be honest with others about what you need to change.

Now it's your turn.

I will no longer tolerate…

1. _____

2. _____

3. _____

4. _____

5. _____

6. _____

7. _____

8. _____

9. _____

10. _____

Dissatisfaction must be present before change can occur. If you aren't dissatisfied with something, why would you change it? As you move through your journey toward your definition of success, you will constantly be confronted by things you need to change. This list gives you a start on the things you want or need to change. The process of change is never ending.

The old cliché says, "The only things certain in this world are death, taxes and change." We usually laugh when we say this but the reality is, it's true. That does not mean that all your life you are going to be unhappy and dissatisfied. What it means is that, as you grow and take action to achieve your goals, you will need to adapt and learn and change in order to make progress.

It is also important for you to recognize those things you may be unhappy with but you cannot change. There are some things in life that are just a brutal fact of your reality. Whether you like it or not, you cannot change it. These are things you will need to accept, and move on with whatever else you need to do. Don't dwell on these issues; just accept them and learn how to work with them or around them.

> *"God, grant me the serenity to accept the things I cannot change, the courage to change the things I can, and the wisdom to know the difference."*
> **– Reinhold Niebuhr**

You cannot re-write your history. If you live in the past, letting your history hold you back, then you are allowing things you cannot change to get in your way.

The problem with living in the past is that we fall victim to the stories of our past and the inability to accept the current reality. Your circumstances of the past are just that, the past. While they may have been very difficult, you have to accept that you cannot change your history. What you can do is change the future you will build. In this case, the change you may need to make is how you allow the past to impact your beliefs, your thoughts and your actions. Move forward toward your dreams by focusing on the future and the success you will achieve.

Identifying areas in your life you are dissatisfied with and have a need to change is absolutely necessary before you can start to make those changes. Understanding those things you cannot change are just as important. Now that you have accomplished both of those things, you need to decide what you will do about it.

Create a Vision of the Outcome You Want

"To exist is to change, to change is to mature, to mature is to go on creating oneself endlessly."
– Henri Bergson

Now that you are ready to embrace change, it's time to create a vision of the outcome of change. In order for change to occur, you need to understand what it's going to look like when the change is made. An easy example is if you have a goal to lose 20 pounds. You can visualize what you will look like when the 20 pounds are gone, what size clothes you will wear, what your spouse or friends will say, and how much better you will feel, etc. Visualizing the end result is important in the change process. Visualizing the outcome you want makes it more real and allows you to understand what you are moving toward.

In 2005, I realized that it was time to make a career change. The bank I had worked for had been bought out by another bank, and the new management and I didn't see eye to eye about how I should lead my team. They had different ideas than I did about how to achieve our goals and what was required to be successful. Banking was no longer for me, and I was ready to make my dream of owning my own business become a reality. I had reached the level of dissatisfaction that made me ready for the change. Before I could make the change though, I needed to set my vision for what I wanted as the outcome from the change.

I certainly didn't know all the details of what my business would look like or how exactly I would do it, but I knew and could visualize what would be different and better after I made the change. There was no way I could have taken the leap of faith to make such a big change in my life if I didn't have a clear vision of what I did want.

Take each of the items you listed earlier in this chapter and ask yourself what your desired outcome is for each area of dissatisfaction you listed. If you need to change a relationship, what do you want from the relationship? If you are going to change your job or career, then decide what you want from the new job or career. If you own a business and need to improve it, what outcome are you looking for? If you are going to start a business, what do you want from that business? What type of lifestyle; what type of work do you want to do; what will be different from your current job?

Identify what your desired outcome is and you will then be ready to take the necessary steps to make the change. Don't underestimate the power of visualization to motivate you. Some of the most successful people in the world use visualization as a way to train or improve their skills.

A friend of mine recently told me about a conversation he had with a member of the Air Force Thunderbirds stunt team. If you have ever seen the Thunderbirds perform, it is amazing. They fly in formations of up to six Air Force F-16 jets at a distance of only a few feet separating each plane from the others in the formation. They perform amazing high-speed aerial stunts synchronizing their flights with great precision. The smallest mistake can create a terrible disaster and the death of one or more pilots. It is a thrill to watch them perform.

The pilot told my friend they practice almost daily using an exercise they call "chair flying." This exercise is completed on the ground in a training room. They close their eyes and visualize every small move of the joystick they need to make to perform each maneuver. Any mistakes are immediately identified so they can correct them while on the ground. Visualization can be an extremely powerful tool in perfecting skills, and it can be used very effectively to help you clearly see what you want to accomplish. Using it will help you overcome the fear of making changes in order to reach success.

Determine Action to Be Taken

In order for any change you make to become permanent, you must take certain steps. It is so easy to revert to the old way of doing things because the old way is comfortable. Real change requires you to stay with it and push through any emotion you have tied to the old way.

Whenever you make meaningful change, some form of emotion always accompanies it. The emotion may be fear because you are not sure what the outcome will be, or if the new way will work or how hard it will be. You may feel stress because you wonder if you are doing it right or how others will perceive you. It could be that you are skeptical or suspicious the new way will even accomplish what you want. You may feel lonely because others you know aren't following the same path, and they may question your motives for making these changes. There are any number of emotions that may come into play as you start making these changes. Don't let emotions keep you from making lasting change.

How many times have you known someone who constantly complained about their lack of money, yet they didn't really know where all their money went? They probably thought over and over again that they needed to get a handle on their finances, yet they never took the steps to do it. There were probably a lot of emotions involved with getting a handle on how they spent their money. There may be fear about finding out they spend too much money on frivolous items like cappuccinos or eating out. They may be stressed about finding out where the money goes because it could require a serious conversation with their spouse about how the money gets spent. They may even believe that there is nothing they can do to make the money last. They simply doubt there is anything they can do about it.

If they are going to make lasting change and get a firm grasp on their finances, they have to set those emotions aside and determine the steps needed to – first – find out how the money is spent and then decide where they can make changes. Setting up a budget and getting some advice may be required. The point is, don't let negative emotions keep you from taking action to make change. Make up your mind that you ARE going to change and that nothing will stop you from achieving your success.

Here are some steps you should take to make a change into a habit and not just a short-term attempt at change.

1. Create a sense of urgency about the change; Change is imperative and failure is not an option.

2. WRITE down specifically what you are trying to change and develop a SMART goal to accomplish it.

3. Identify any obstacle that could get in your way.

4. WRITE out a plan to overcome each of the obstacles you have identified.

5. WRITE out your vision of what you are trying to accomplish by making the change and what it will look like when the change is accomplished – be specific.

6. Check to insure the change you are contemplating will get you closer to your definition of success. If it does, go after it with a passion. If it doesn't, go back and adjust what you need to change to get back in alignment.

7. Share it with your mentor or coach.

Remember that writing all of this down is necessary and will help you commit to the change. Just telling yourself you will do it is not enough. Make the commitment to write it down, share it with your mentor or coach and ask them to hold you accountable to doing it. Once you have made this level of commitment to change, then you are almost assured of making it happen and making the change stick.

Don't forget to reward yourself along the way. As you make progress and lock in the new habits you are forming while making the needed changes, take time to give yourself a reward for sticking to it and getting closer to the success you want. The rewards don't have to be big and shouldn't be tied to what you are changing so you don't sabotage the process, but they should allow you to recognize your accomplishment. You deserve to reward yourself, but doing this also gives you motivation to continue making the changes necessary to get your bad habits out of the way and live the life of your dreams.

Summary

"They always say time changes things, but you actually have to change them yourself."
– Andy Warhol

Now that you know how to accept and embrace change in your life, you should no longer have a fear of change or be resistant to making the changes needed to achieve success. Understanding that it is up to you to make the life you want and that you will need to make change a way of life is critical to your success. Don't wait for the things you are unhappy with or don't want to tolerate any longer to change themselves. You will be waiting a long time. Take control of creating the life you want and making the changes needed to get you there.

You must be willing to apply new remedies, or you can expect to continue getting the same results and continue to be dissatisfied with your progress toward success.

By asking yourself what the things are that you will no longer tolerate in your life, you will be able to identify what you need to change. You must be totally honest with yourself to completely remove the obstacles getting in your way. You can do all the work to identify what success means to you, create your vision, and set your goals, and define your self-limiting beliefs and still have a difficult time achieving your success if you aren't willing to make changes.

You will need to change what you are doing today, and you will need to remain open to change as you progress toward your goals. The world we are living in today will not be the same world tomorrow, next year or ten years from now. Change is constant and your ability to embrace change and adopt change as a way of life will make your journey toward success a much smoother and faster road.

Start the change process by identifying one item on your list of items that you will no longer tolerate, that you feel confident about changing, and do it. Once you have accomplished this change, then move on to another item on the list and do the same thing. Once you have a few successes under your belt, you will gain confidence in your ability to handle more difficult changes or to identify and handle future changes.

You are now making significant progress toward achieving the success you want from life. You will become unstoppable when you adopt an attitude of change and remove any self-limiting beliefs you have that have kept you from making changes in your life.

CHAPTER 10

Don't Just Talk About It; Do It

"It is in your moments of decision that your destiny is shaped."
- Anthony Robbins

When I say the word "action," what comes to mind? Is your first reaction that it sounds like a lot of work? So many times the perfect plans we make are sabotaged by our lack of action. We can dream and plan and even set goals for our life, but when it comes time to put them into action, we hesitate or give up. So far you have invested a lot of time thinking about what you want from life and making plans for it. But now it's time to take action on those plans and make your dreams come true.

It's time to quit talking about what you dream of having in life and start doing something about it. The world doesn't reward you for talking about something; it rewards you for what you do. The axiom of success states, "The universe rewards action." It is surprising how many people are bogged down in talking about it, analyzing, planning and organizing but never taking the first step.

You now understand what self-limiting beliefs are and what you need to do to remove them from your path. You have identified the action steps you need to take by determining your self-limiting beliefs, finding a mentor for support, identifying the learning you must do and by accepting change as a way of life. Now you must to be willing to take positive action to turn it all into success. All that we have discussed so far is pointless if you don't take action.

Action can feel like work to many people. But if your actions are inspired by your passions and dreams, then it will become effortless. Inspired action isn't really work because it leads you to your dream. Taking action leads to the accomplishment of your goals, but if you fail to take action, you are just a dreamer. Talk is cheap and will earn you nothing but disappointment. You will not achieve the success you desire and will spend your time wondering why you are not getting what you want from life.

I simply cannot express enough how important it is for you to move forward a little bit every day. Action is the secret to success. There has been a lot of talk in recent years about the law of attraction and how to use it to get what you want from life. Many experts tell you to think positively and believe you will succeed and you will attract success to you. It has been documented over and over again throughout history about the power of positive thinking, and there is no doubt there is some truth to it. I don't want to downplay at all the power of having a positive attitude and expecting good things to happen. I consider the law of attraction to be a key ingredient in helping you achieve success.

However, thinking positively and focusing on what you want will not lead you to success by itself. Maintaining a positive attitude and believing good things will come your way is very powerful when combined with positive action. If you spend the next 90 days sitting on your couch all day thinking as positively as you possibly can, what do you think will happen? Go ahead, get up nice and early, have some cereal and then go sit on the couch until it is time to go to bed. Do nothing but think about what you want from life and how you are going to feel with all your new money and possessions. Do that for 90 days and what will you get?

I am exaggerating the whole process to make a point. Just thinking about it won't make it happen. Your bank account won't magically start to grow, your relationships won't improve themselves, your weight won't disappear and you won't automatically achieve your other goals.

Let me give you an example of the power of taking positive action on your dreams. Mary Kay Ash was born on May 12, 1918, in Houston, Texas. Her parents encouraged her to succeed and always told her, "You can do it." When she began her career, she moved to Dallas, Texas and took a part-time job with Stanley Home Products selling household goods at parties in women's homes. She focused on improving her sales skills and would write weekly sales goals in soap on her bathroom mirror.

In 1949, she joined another direct-sales company, World Gifts, as national sales director. But in 1963, the company promoted a male colleague who had been hired in as her assistant over her at twice the salary she was making. Mary Kay felt the men managing the company didn't believe that a woman could succeed. She told *Texas Monthly* magazine in 1995, "Those men didn't believe a woman had brain matter at all. I learned back then that as long as men didn't believe women could do anything, women were never going to have a chance."

So Mary Kay took action and left World Gifts to begin thinking about what she could do to help empower women to succeed. She had a passion for helping women get ahead. She made the decision that, if she was going to reach the success she knew she was capable of and see her vision of helping women in their careers, she needed to start her own business. Her efforts led to the founding of Mary Kay Cosmetics. She said to herself, "Why are you theorizing about a dream company? Why don't you just start one?" And that is exactly what she did. She didn't just think about it and dream about it, she took action, accepted the risk and did it.

In fact, she did it so well that her company grew from a sales force of 11 in 1963 to more than 750,000 in 37 countries with wholesale revenue of more than $1.3 billion in 2000. She created a company that has inspired countless women to become their own boss and go into the direct-sales business. More than 150 women have earned at least $1 million working for Mary Kay. She had a vision to create a company that empowered women to take control of their own life and their own success. Numerous women have earned the famous pink Cadillac as well as items such as mink coats, diamond rings and other awards for their success.

Now, if Mary Kay had just stayed at World Gifts and complained about how unfair the bosses were, think about how many women would not have achieved the level of success they have by being a part of the Mary Kay company. Or, if she had just talked about creating a company to help women but never took action to make it happen, those 150 women that earned over $1 million might not be wealthy today. No one would have rewarded her for thinking about it or talking about it. But she was rewarded, not just with immense wealth, but also with the satisfaction that she made a huge difference in the lives of hundreds of thousands of women around the world. She is quoted as saying, "I wasn't that interested in the dollars and cents part of business. My interest in starting Mary Kay, Inc. was to offer women opportunities that didn't exist anywhere else." She achieved her definition of success because she took action to make it happen.

You need to think positively and believe with all your heart and soul that you will succeed and then go for it! Good things will happen because you have the right attitude, beliefs and drive to make it happen. Knowing the actions you are taking are moving you closer to what you want in life will make it easier to do what you need to do.

Eating the Elephant One Bite at a Time

"Step by step. I can't see any other way of accomplishing anything."
– Michael Jordan

When you look at what you wrote as your definition of success and your vision statements, do you feel a little overwhelmed? Does it seem like a very large leap to get there from where you are today? Don't worry. You don't need to try to get there in one big leap. Your journey to success will be a progression of thousands of little steps. It's like eating an elephant. When you look at the elephant you think, "Man, there is no way I am going to be able to eat that whole thing." The only way to do it is to take one bite at a time since you certainly can't swallow it whole!

Vision without action is simply a daydream, but trying to tackle too much at one time is simply unrealistic.

You still have your daily life you need to live. Going to work each day, taking care of your family, your home, all your other responsibilities, plus having some fun along the way still needs to happen. You can't just put everything in your life on hold while you pursue your goals. This can be done in conjunction with everything else you have to do. You will still be able to achieve unlimited success by taking one-step at a time.

In the *John Whitmore* book, *Coaching for Performance,* he tells the story of John Nabor and his incredible journey to Olympic history. It all started in 1972 when a young swimmer by the name of John Nabor watched Mark Spitz win an amazing seven gold medals for swimming in the Munich Olympics. After watching Spitz win, Nabor decided he too would win an Olympic gold medal. He wanted to win his medal in the 100- meter backstroke. He set a goal to accomplish this in the 1976 Montreal Olympics.

Nabor had already won the National Junior Championship, but he was still nearly five seconds off the pace he knew was necessary to win the gold. Now five seconds doesn't sound like much, but when you are competing at that level of competition, it is a huge deficit to make up. Undaunted, Nabor decided to break his goal down into manageable steps. He began by asking himself how much he would need to improve in each practice session to achieve his goal. By taking the number of hours he could practice over the next four years before the Olympics and dividing it into the number of seconds he needed to improve he arrived at his goal. His goal – he needed to improve by one- fifth of one eye blink for every hour of training. That's right, one fifth of one eye blink an hour. Suddenly he had a goal he could understand and accept as doable. So, he worked diligently and hard over the next four years improving one little bit at each training session.

By 1976, he had improved so much that he was made the captain of the American swimming team, and he won not just one gold medal, but two. He won the gold medal for the 100- meter backstroke and the 200-meter backstroke, the first one in a new world record time and the second in a new Olympic record. He ate the elephant one small bite at a time and exceeded his goal. He achieved his dream and created the success he sought. Nabor was motivated by an end goal he was passionate about and chose a process that created a path for him to achieve success.

"The journey of a thousand miles begins with a single step."
– Lao-tzu, Chinese Philosopher

You need to take responsibility to determine how you will break your goals down. Remember, you must take your long-term goals and break them down into 90-day objectives. Each 90-day plan will take you a step closer to your end goal. You get to choose how you will break them down further to what you need to do each day. Every morning ask yourself, "What can I do *today* to make positive momentum toward my 90-day objectives?" Breaking the goals into small steps will get you there with an ease you never expected. The action you take will not be hard work; it will be exciting and fulfilling. Your positive attitude and belief in yourself, along with your satisfaction at seeing progress, will make you proud and give you the motivation and courage to continue along your path toward success.

Add an extra 15 minutes each day to the time you invest in yourself and working on your success plan, and you will have added an equivalent of more than two weeks each year to the achievement of your dreams.

Imagine the exponentially powerful progress you will make by taking 15 minutes away from watching television, or surfing the internet or even sleeping and applying it to developing the life you want. Imagine what would happen if you invested an hour or more each day to your success plan! This is an investment that cannot be matched by any other thing you can possibly do. Invest more in yourself than you do in your business or career, and you will see everything in your life move in the right direction.

Make an extra contact knowledgeable in the area you are working on improving, or read another book, or attend another workshop, or anything that gets you closer to where you want to go. The important thing is just to do a little more each day and the rewards will be great.

Procrastination Is an Assassin of Opportunity

"Procrastination is the thief of time."
– **Edward Young**

Have you ever gone to work and had a big project or something you needed to do to help you achieve your goals, and you just couldn't manage to get yourself started on it? Maybe you had a report due to your boss or a major customer you needed to call on. You got to work and figured you would just check your email quickly, then the phone rings and then someone stops by your office to chat for a while. Next thing you know it's time for lunch, and you still haven't started your project. Oh well, no sense in digging into it and then having to stop for lunch, you might as well wait until you get back. Half a day is shot and you have now managed to avoid doing that one thing you told yourself was so important.

Does this sound like you? Do you find yourself saying things like, "I'll feel more like doing this tomorrow," or "I work best under pressure," or maybe you look at your list of things to do and say something like, "This isn't very important, it can wait." Procrastinators tend to lie to themselves to feel better.

If you want to see some major procrastination, then ask someone to make some telemarketing calls. I always get a kick out of how many excuses people can come up with to avoid picking up the phone. Another great one is when it's time to start a weight loss program. The idea of starting on a diet isn't very appealing so there is always a reason why we should wait until tomorrow to start. In my hometown, we had a Joe's Crab Shack Restaurant, and on the side of the building was painted, "Free Crabs tomorrow!" The problem is tomorrow never arrived, so I've been waiting for those free crabs for a long time now. Unfortunately, the same is true for many people that have dreams of changing their life but always wait for tomorrow to start.

There is absolutely no better time to get started on creating the life you want and achieving success than right now!

Successful people show more self-discipline than other people do. They develop good habits like organization skills, persistence and priority-management skills. Force yourself to keep your commitments to yourself and others, and you will see the day when you keep them very efficiently without even needing to think about it. Do the same with the goals you have established. Each day, set out your priorities; the one or two things from your 90-day planner you will work on that day. Make this list of priorities a non-negotiable "to do," and after a while it will become a habit. It will simply become a way of life for you. Self-discipline is key to eliminating procrastination from your life.

More than 20 percent of people identify themselves as chronic procrastinators. Add in the need to make changes or take steps you are not accustomed to taking and that number goes way up. When it is time to do something new or to take action that is not comfortable for you, it is a natural reaction to put it off. To overcome the comfort of procrastination, you first need to believe absolutely you can and will achieve success. The right mind-set is the first step. Once you have set your mind on taking action, then you must commit to getting out of your own way and move forward each day.

Do not let procrastination steal your dreams from you. After all the work you have done to move you toward success, it would be a real shame to let procrastination assassinate that effort. This is another very important reason why you need to have a coach or mentor working with you along your journey. Make sure that any mentor you choose is willing to push you and hold you accountable to making progress and not let you get away with just thinking about it and not taking the action required. A coach or mentor should be willing to push you, if necessary, to the point where you become angry. Sometimes it is necessary to use anger and frustration to get you back on track.

In Michael Jordan's biography, he talks about the need to stay focused on your goals and put in the work required to achieve your desired outcome. Michael says, "I've always believed that if you put in the work, the results will come. I don't do things half-heartedly. Because I know if I do, then I can expect halfhearted results." Michael understood that, if you want to achieve real success, you have to be willing to do the work and take action. But a lot of people still approach their goals and their life halfheartedly. They keep waiting for tomorrow or some other time to actually begin doing what they need to do. He went on to say, "That's why a lot of people fail. They sound like they're committed to being the best they can be. They say all the right things and make all the proper appearances. But when it comes right down to it, they're looking for reasons instead of answers."

Taking action every day and not looking for reasons why you should wait or why you can't do it now is the sign of a mind-set of success. Time is a precious commodity and is limited in its supply. Each day you let pass without taking another step forward is a lost opportunity. Remove from your mind any thought of waiting until later and take action now. Each day you move forward and work toward eliminating your self-limiting beliefs is getting you closer to success in your life.

Setting Milestones

Let's pretend you have set a goal to become your own boss. You want to own your own business and give up having someone else always telling you what to do and working really hard to meet their goals instead of your own. It's time to start building the life you want, and being your own boss is one of the paths you have chosen. You have written on your vision statement to be a business owner, and you have set a goal to make it happen. Today though, you are still working for someone else, and you know it is going to take a lot of work to make your business a success.

Take it a step at a time and do not try to get it all done at once. In order to make the process of breaking it into steps easier, establish milestones that allow you to measure your progress. Milestones are simply points along the path to achieving a goal that allow you to measure your progress. Milestones allow you to create reference points that mark major events in a project. They are used to monitor the project's progress. Your vision statements and goals are milestones on your path toward your definition of success. Your 90-day objectives are milestones. Each measurable goal you write using the SMART formula is getting you a little closer to success. They are milestones you can recognize when you have reached them.

One of the greatest gaps in life is the gap between knowing what you need to do and actually doing it. Setting goals and establishing milestones gives you the motivation to take action.

Use milestones as a way to keep you on track and establish points at which you will reward yourself. Set a specific reward for yourself tied to a specific milestone. If your first milestone in opening your own business is the date that you finish your business plan and financial projections, assign a reward to it that will motivate you to keep moving toward the next milestone.

Take Action, Verify Then Take More Action

Be sure that as you move forward, you keep checking back against your definition of success and your vision statements to make sure you have not strayed from your path. Life gets in the way at times and tends to push us in different directions. It is so easy to get distracted by all the other things you have to do that, when you finally take a break and look back at your dreams, you find that you have drifted off track.

By setting the 90-day objectives and working on them diligently each day, you will find that you are less likely to get off track. Nevertheless, pull out your written definition of success and your written vision statement and review them to make sure you have not drifted off somewhere along the way. It will be a big relief to you to know that you are making positive progress toward the life you want.

"Never mistake motion for action."
– Ernest Hemingway

Just because you are doing "stuff" doesn't mean that you are making progress toward the right objectives. Making sure the action you are taking is the right action is important to make sure you are not wasting time. Focused action is so very powerful. Stay focused and you will be amazed at how much you can accomplish.

Summary

*"Success is a ladder that cannot be climbed
with your hands in your pockets."*
— **American Proverb**

Success will not be handed to you and it will not come to you just because you think about it. Developing and maintaining an attitude of success is extremely important. If you believe with all your heart that you will succeed and focus on things you need to help you achieve success, then you will begin to attract those things to you. Thought alone will not get you to success. Action is required, and you need to be willing to commit to take action every day along your journey.

The quality of the life you lead is directly related to the quality of the decisions you make and the action you take.

You will achieve amazing results if you simply adopt a mind-set of action. Create strong habits of doing something every single day that gets you closer to your desired outcome of success. Since the majority of people prefer to procrastinate instead of actually doing what they talk about, you will find that you will start to stand out from the crowd. People will start to wonder what you are doing differently that is making you so successful. When that happens, don't let them influence you and discourage you from doing what you need to do. Keep focused and do what you need to, and you will get the life and/or business of your dreams.

Don't try to do it all at once. Understand that taking it a step at a time is the right way to approach it. Step-by-step is amazingly powerful when it becomes your way of life. You will find that in a year you have accomplished more than you had expected. Momentum will start to build as you begin to see some of your short-term goals accomplished. It is such a good feeling to begin checking things off your 90-day planner and to know that you are making progress.

Your coach or mentor should be an accountability partner to help keep you on track and taking action. When we are accountable to someone else for our actions, we tend to take them much more seriously and don't want to tell the other person that we didn't do what we said we would. Commit to having an accountability partner and demand that they hold you to your plan. You will thank them in the end and find that they were an integral factor in your success.

I want to end this section with two final points. It simply is not enough to want it, or to dream about it or even to talk about it. If you want success, you must do what it takes to get there. Benjamin Franklin said:

"Well done is better than well said."

The last point is that you need to commit in writing to taking action. Once you commit to it in writing and post it where you can see it often, it will act as a reminder for you. Once taking action toward your stated mission becomes a habit, you will find that it just starts to happen naturally. Until then, keep the reminder in front of you. On the following page is an action commitment statement for you to sign and post. Placing your signature on the line means you agree to take the action to create your dream life including the business or career you want. Take time now to sign it and post it.

Your dream of success is within your grasp. Take the action required to claim the life you want.

ACHIEVING UNLIMITED SUCCESS

Action Commitment Statement for

_____

(your name)

I commit to taking action every day toward my goals to create the life of my dreams. I understand that in order to get what I want from life I need to do new things. I will identify the next step in my plan and stay focused on doing what is needed to achieve success in that step and then move on to the next step in the process. I understand that success is a journey that requires constant focus and dedication to my dreams, and I am willing to do what it takes to get there.

Committed to this _____ day of _____

by _____

CHAPTER 11

Stay Committed
to Your Plan

*"The miracle or the power that elevates the
few is found in their perseverance under the
prompting of a brave determined spirit."*
— **Mark Twain**

Have you ever had something special planned that you really wanted to go just perfectly? You probably worried that it would not go right and your special event would be ruined. You did everything you could to make sure it turned out just the way you wanted it. Maybe you dreamed for a long time about a special vacation. Maybe it was a weeklong cruise or a trip to Hawaii that you were excited about taking. How about your wedding day? Think of all the planning and preparation that went into that one day.

What if you hired a wedding planner to handle things for you and the planner wasn't committed to doing the job? She didn't return your phone calls or show up for meetings. She decided to take the week before your wedding to go on vacation and left details unattended. How would you feel about that wedding planner? What would you do to make sure the wedding went the way you wanted it?

Of course, what you would do is fire the wedding planner, not pay her and take over the planning yourself or find a different planner. You wouldn't just sit by and take the attitude that it wasn't a big deal. You would take control and do everything you could to see to it your wedding was a day to remember. No matter what your budget was and how elaborate or simple the wedding, you certainly would want it to be perfect.

Why is it that we will be 100 percent committed to making sure events like vacations, weddings and parties come off perfect, but we don't take the same interest in making sure our business and life come out exactly the way we want it? Of course, the events mentioned above are short-term in nature and, after a lot of work in a little amount of time, we have a great event that people remember. Working on your life is a long-term project but can be extremely rewarding.

Those who are most successful at creating the business and life they want are the ones who commit 100 percent to their plan. Those that say the right things but then don't do what they say they are going to do don't achieve their goals. You already understand the importance of taking action. The next step is to be totally committed to following through with your plans.

Commitment can be difficult for some people who have an aversion to or fear of it. Their reasoning is that they like their freedom and see committing to anything as taking away some of that freedom. By committing to a certain path and saying "yes" to doing specific things, they are, by definition, saying "no" to something else. Because we all have a finite amount of time, any time you say "yes" you are saying "no" to something else. So, if you have committed to attending an educational workshop to enhance your business skills, you are saying no to doing something else with that time. If you choose to have lunch with your mentor to discuss your progress, then you are saying no to lunch with your friend from the office.

In order to commit to attaining your goals, you have to make those choices. To be committed to success, you need to have the capacity to pledge yourself to a result worth creating. If your definition of success is truly one that you believe with all your heart is worth creating, then it will be easy to make the commitment to it. It is through commitment to your goals that you create what matters most in your life. This includes your business, relationships, wealth, status and any other components of your success definition you want to create.

You will be better able to navigate life's messy complexities and find the way to real, lasting and meaningful fulfillment by showing the determination and commitment to achieving your goals without letting anything get in your way. Keep your goals and plans simple, and you will find it easier to stay disciplined. Life's treasures can be accomplished by maintaining the right mental focus, remaining determined and committed to achieving success, and keeping your plans simple and straightforward. We tend to make life more complicated than it has to be. The experts tell us we need to employ difficult and costly strategies to our business and career problems. We love to believe that life is difficult and therefore the solutions must be difficult.

The reality is, with determination, commitment and belief that success is inevitable, you will achieve greater success than you previously thought possible.

Take Wilma Rudolph as an example of determination and commitment leading to success. Wilma was born in Clarksville, Tennessee, in 1940. She was born prematurely and weighed only 4.5 pounds. Wilma's mother spent the first several years nursing her through one illness after another. At the age of four, she had double pneumonia with scarlet fever. She had to be taken to a doctor and it was discovered that her left leg and foot were becoming weak and deformed. She was told she had polio, a crippling disease that had no cure. The doctor told her mother that Wilma would never walk. Mrs. Rudolph refused to give up on Wilma and found treatment for her. She made Wilma believe she could do anything she wanted if she only believed. Wilma started doing physical therapy exercises at home and by the time she was twelve years old she could walk normally. It was then that she decided to become an athlete.

Wilma said, "I want to be the fastest woman on this earth," and set herself on a path to do just that. At the age of thirteen, she took part in her first race and finished in last place, way behind the other racers. She didn't give up but continued to believe in herself and stayed determined to reach her goal. She continued to enter other races and to finish in last place. Then one day she entered a race where she finished first. At the age of fifteen, she went to Tennessee State University, where she met a coach and shared her goal to become the fastest women on this earth. Her coach told her that with her spirit she could not be stopped.

In the 1960 Olympics, Wilma Rudolph, the paralytic girl, became the fastest woman in the world by winning three Olympic Gold medals. She won the 100-meter dash, the 200-meter dash and ran the anchor leg of the 400-meter relay team. This achievement led her to become one of the most celebrated female athletes of all time.

No one would suggest that Wilma's journey to success was easy. She had to work very hard and overcome amazing obstacles to reach her dream of success. By staying committed to her goal and taking a positive step each day and through her training and determination, she lived her dream. She didn't need complicated strategies to succeed but instead worked hard, believed in herself and her dream, and was determined to reach her goal. You can do the same thing with the right level of desire and commitment to make it happen.

Perseverance

"Many of life's failures are men who did not realize how close they were to success when they gave up."
— **Thomas Edison**

So many times people give up too early on their dreams. There will come a point during your journey where you will feel discouraged and consider giving up. Unfortunately, life does not always proceed as we wish it would. There will be challenging times with obstacles you cannot foresee. When those times happen, you have to make a choice. Pressure and stress will build as you run into these obstacles, and you have the choice to run away and quit, giving up on the life you want, or to push through the obstacles. There will be some type of emotion tied to these obstacles. It might be fear, doubt, anxiety or any number of emotions. Understand that this will happen, but you cannot let it deter you from your goals.

Perseverance and failure are not able to exist together. Failure only occurs when you decide to give up. Perseverance overcomes failure when you refuse to quit. Another major key to solidifying your commitment is to persevere by refusing to give up. Your goals and dreams deserve all the effort and commitment you can give them.

Even when you feel like you have been knocked down, you need to get up and keep going. Some people refer to this as having "stick-to-itiveness." Think about all the times during your life when you refused to quit. When you were learning to ride a bike, you probably fell down but got right back up and tried again. You refused to stop trying and eventually learned how to ride. Apply that same stick-to-itiveness to pursuing your dreams.

"Never, Never, Never, Never Give Up."
– Winston Churchill

The world is full of examples of people who started a business and tried to make it successful. After they ran into some difficulty, they chose to give up. Instead of finding answers or seeking guidance, they quit. They accepted failure and went back to working for someone else. There are also many examples of people who started businesses and overcame adversity to build great companies. These people had to persevere through tough times to build their company. They chose to stay with it and work through the challenges and were rewarded for it.

There are countless examples of people who persevered despite failing many times. Take the story of a boy nicknamed Sparky. Throughout his youth, he was awkward socially. He struggled throughout school and failed every subject in eighth grade. During high school he was afraid of rejection, so he never once asked a girl for a date.

Sparky, used to failing and being rejected, accepted that he was a loser. The one thing Sparky really loved was drawing. He was proud of his artwork even though no one else really appreciated it. In his senior year, he submitted some cartoon drawings to the editors of his yearbook. They were rejected.

When he graduated from high school, he wrote a letter to Walt Disney Studios. He was told to send some samples of a cartoon, and he spent considerable time drawing them. When he finally received his reply from the Disney Studios he was once again rejected.

Sparky decided to write his own biography in cartoons. He described his childhood in the cartoons. How he could never seem to kick the football or get his kite to fly. How he was a chronic underachiever. His cartoons went on to become the most famous cartoon of all time with his character *Charlie Brown!*

Sparky, the boy who could never seem to win, was Charles Schulz. He was rejected repeatedly, but because he knew his passion and pursued it, he ended up winning. Charles Schulz persevered and succeeded even beyond his dreams. Because Schulz wouldn't give up, the world was blessed with his wonderful cartoons. He is quoted as saying, "Well, frankly I did expect it (success), because it was something I had planned for since I was six years old." Through all his difficulties, he never gave up on his dream.

You show perseverance by spending time focusing on those things that will lead you to success. An example is giving up things that are not helping you and working on those that will. You can choose to spend less money on things that don't fit into your goals and decide to invest in things that will. You persevere if you study, work hard and try again at something you were not successful at the first time. When you overcome adversity to achieve a goal, you are showing the perseverance needed to win. Perseverance is being able to bear difficulties calmly and without complaint. It is trying again and again until you succeed.

Failure is the path of least resistance. Choosing to accept failure instead of pushing through the failure is the easy way out. It may be hard to keep moving forward but doing so shows determination and commitment. You may be disappointed if you fail, but your dreams are doomed if you do not keep trying. No one can keep your success from you except you.

Determination can be a very powerful enemy of failure. If you are determined enough to reach your goals, then the idea of accepting failure will not even occur to you.

Whatever your goals are, you need to stick to them. Your vision of success creates a mental picture of the life you are striving for. Keep that picture in mind whenever you run into difficulty. By doing this, it will be easier to keep working at it instead of giving up.

There are so many examples of people who had a vision of their dream and stayed focused on making it a reality. Mark Victor Hansen had been working with his partner Jack Canfield on a book of inspirational stories for quite some time. They presented the idea for their inspirational book to publisher after publisher and were rejected by 140 book publishers. They remained determined to see their vision become a reality and, today, the *Chicken Soup* series has sold over 100 million copies. When Harland Sanders was 62 years old, he decided to franchise his unique recipe for southern fried chicken and traveled the country selling his idea. He barely had more than his $105 Social Security payment at the time, so he drove himself around the country cooking up a batch of his famous chicken for restaurant owners and entering into agreements with them to sell his chicken. Harland Sanders became known as Colonel Sanders, and the Kentucky Fried Chicken business he founded is known worldwide. Harland decided he was not going to give up and sit around living on social security, and his determination created a very successful business.

These are just two people who refused to quit and pushed through the frustration and rejection they encountered. The point is simply that you should never give up.

"Effort only releases its reward after
a person refuses to quit."
– Napoleon Hill

Giving up is not an option to someone who has clearly defined what they want to achieve and the steps they need to take to get there.

Self-Discipline

We have talked about staying focused on what you want until it is yours. By staying focused on the bigger picture, there may be times when you need to deny yourself small things until you can achieve the big goal you really want. That is what self-discipline is all about. It is important to recognize that our mind plays tricks on us. Sometimes it will attempt to divert us from achieving our goal when it looks too much like work. Sometimes we stall our own best efforts by not practicing self-discipline.

Learning to be self-disciplined helps to nip this problem in the bud. So, what does self-discipline mean? It is the ability to do things we need to do even when we don't really feel like doing it. The hardest part is staying focused on doing what needs done. The good thing about developing self-discipline is that it is fairly easy to train your mind to it. It can be compared to training a muscle. When you exercise it on a regular basis, it becomes strong and healthy. On the other hand, if left unused, it will weaken and atrophy.

Self-discipline is built from habits and repetitive patterns of behavior. When you establish a pattern of achieving your goals, it creates momentum. This makes it easier to stay committed to your objectives. After you have experienced the satisfaction of completing a few of your goals, you will be more disciplined. You will want to achieve the next goal and then the next goal until you have reached your dreams. Show self-discipline toward the goals you have set, and you will have the outcome you are aiming for sooner instead of later.

Begin to use self-discipline today to increase your level of commitment. Say no to those things that will try to de-rail you from your path. Instead, remain focused on what you are working on and stay committed to the end objective. Use self-discipline to work on your goals, and you will find your level of commitment increasing. Don't let a lack of self-discipline cause you to lose momentum and decrease your level of commitment.

Risk versus Reward Analysis

Any path you choose will have a variety of risk and rewards. Of course, the ultimate reward will be achieving the success you are working toward. Throughout the journey to success, you will be making risk reward assessments. The analysis should be to look at the objectives you have set for each 90-day period and verify they align with your ultimate goal of success. This exercise will help to increase your level of commitment providing encouragement that you are on the right track.

When you compare the action you are currently undertaking to a long-term goal, the positive feelings associated with those dreams are reinforced. Stirring these feelings helps to increase the power of the vision you have of your ideal life. The reward you are giving yourself will outweigh the risk of taking the step you are committing to get you closer to your goal.

Of course, if you do this risk reward analysis and determine the step you are about to start doesn't get you closer to your objective, then you will determine not to do it. Don't forget about the importance of giving yourself small rewards as you accomplish certain milestones. The determination of the rewards you will receive by taking action against your goals will dramatically increase your commitment to taking the needed action.

Focused Attention

You get what you focus on in life. By controlling our attention, we are able to control our outcomes. By focusing our attention on what it is we want in life, we are keeping it off the things we do not want. Whenever you find yourself beginning to drift away from the things you want to accomplish in life, then re-focus your attention.

Your short-term goals help you determine areas in your life to focus on for the purpose of achieving that goal. It can be any of the goals you have established including financial, spiritual, mental, physical or educational in nature. Select one specific area and decide that you are going to focus your attention on it today in order to understand how you are creating improvement or change there.

If it is financial, focus your attention on how your money is spent by keeping records to review. If it is spiritual, determine where you need to focus your attention to better connect spiritually. If it is mental, determine what is causing the mental concern and seek advice about overcoming this concern. If it is physical, ask yourself what you need to do to improve the physical situation and create a plan. If it is educational, determine what book, program, class, job or other format will provide the knowledge and focus on completing it. A strong focused approach to taking the steps you have outlined in your success plan will keep you committed to them.

Strong Mission + Strong Vision + Plan of Action + FOCUS = Success

Focus your attention first thing in the morning to set your mental focus for the day. Do it again at bedtime to lock in the progress you made during the day. This allows your mental state to stay focused on the positives. You achieve what you focus on, so keep your thoughts locked in on what you want and what you have achieved. Be pulled into action each day by keeping positive focused attention on your expected outcomes.

It Won't Be Perfect the First Time

What was it like the first time you tried to get a job? Not the job that you worked at during the summer between school years, but the first full time job you applied for that began your work career. Did you just walk into the company's office, tell them you wanted a job and they gave you one on the spot? Once you did get a job, was it the perfect job that you were going to spend the rest of your career at? The fact is, you probably had to apply to several companies and go on multiple interviews to get a good job. Unless you were extremely fortunate, your first job was probably not the perfect one you would never think of leaving.

Normally when you are trying to make a major change in your life, everything does not happen perfectly the first time. To find your first job or to find a new job, you will go through a process of trial and error. You'll contact some companies that don't have an opening for a position. You will interview for some positions that will be given to someone else, not you. That will not deter you, though, from continuing to look for a job you are interested in doing. The same thing will happen on your journey toward success.

Not everything you attempt will work out the way you might hope it would. There will be some disappointments along the way and you should expect it. You may choose to do some things you think will get you the education or skills or experience you need only to find out that it didn't quite fill the need. You will need to adjust and keep moving forward putting the unsuccessful experience behind you.

Experience and advice will help you avoid losing your determination to succeed if you keep the perspective that your journey will not be a perfect progression of learning. The ability to keep things in perspective and learning from ALL your experiences will be a great asset to you. There are too many times when people let a setback discourage them.

Some time ago I met with a business owner who wanted to make changes in his company. As we started to develop a relationship, it became apparent he was very reliant on a key team member to keep the business successful. Shortly after we met, the key team member left the business to start his own business. The owner was so devastated, he decided to give up on his dream of growing the business. Instead he chose to keep doing things the same way he had always done them in the past. Granted, the loss of this key team member was a major setback, but it should not have derailed the owner from pursuing his own dream. He simply was not determined enough to achieve his dream. Don't let this happen to you.

If you truly are passionate about achieving the success you desire, you will take these experiences as simple detours along the path and not as roadblocks that can't be overcome. Your desire, determination and commitment to building the best life for you will carry you through these setbacks, and you will learn to accept them and move on.

Summary

"Desire is the key to motivation, but it is determination and commitment to an unrelenting pursuit of your goal – a commitment to excellence – that will enable you to attain the success you seek."
– **Mario Andretti**

Building a strong level of commitment to your goals will move you along the path to your vision of success. You must be 100 percent committed to doing whatever it takes to build the life of your dreams. If you are struggling to take action on the goals you set, then go back and review your definition of success. Make adjustments to it if necessary to get you on the right track. By taking time up front to develop a strong life mission and vision, you will find it much easier to commit.

You have defined the desired outcome for your life, what may get in the way and what steps you need to take to overcome those obstacles. You have committed to taking action on those plans. Therefore, there is really nothing that should stop you now. As long as you are truly committed to your course of action and keep focused on the rewards you will achieve in life, then you are unstoppable.

CHAPTER 12

Removing the Head Trash

"Formulate and stamp indelibly on your mind a mental picture of yourself as succeeding. Hold this picture tenaciously and never permit it to fade. Your mind will seek to develop this picture!"
— Dr. Norman Vincent Peale

How many times has that little voice in your head kept you from doing something you wanted to do? It's the voice that tells you what you are about to do is not a good idea. We all have that little voice that creeps into our thinking when we are about to do something uncomfortable. Learn to use that inner voice to help you make progress through active thought.

One of the greatest tools you have for achieving success is within you. It is the power of active thought. Controlling what you think and how you think. Your ability to remove negative thoughts and replace them with positive thoughts that lead to taking the actions you need is a great gift. Your mind is capable of solving any challenge you give it. Your thoughts and your will power reside in your mind. You can program it like a computer to do, think and react however you want it to. Most people do not use the mind in such an active way and, instead, let their thoughts control them thus creating the head trash that holds us back.

Here is a little exercise to help illustrate this.

Lift your left hand and touch your right ear very lightly. Now that you have completed that task, I want you to answer the following question. How did you make your left hand touch your right ear? Think about it for a moment. You will probably say something like, "I just did it." The movement you made was from a conscious thought. It was the consequence of thinking about taking that action and commanding your mind to signal the part of your brain responsible for this action. You have the power in you to tell your mind what you want to do and think. Your mind does not just randomly tell your hand to move to your ear, to take a step or to drive a car. You command your mind to do this and it follows your orders.

The same is true for taking action in your life to achieve the life you want. You can choose to tell your mind to think positive thoughts and take positive action or not. Head trash is placed in your mind by you and not by anyone else.

A recent newsletter for public speaking professionals offered an interesting free tele-seminar. It was for speakers who had the fear that, one day, someone was going to wake up and discover they were not any smarter than the people they were presenting to. It is a common fear among public speakers that they are no more qualified to speak from the front of the room than anyone else there. Even though they have years of experience and a gift for delivering a message, they still have these negative thoughts.

This is an example of head trash. It is when you create doubt or fear that has no basis in fact. This creates a self-limiting belief that must be removed. It is not possible to completely eliminate this type of thinking from your life. Instead, you must control it through the use of active thought. You must recognize what it is when it happens and train your mind to change your thoughts stopping the head trash.

Another example of head trash commonly occurs when it is time to make a telemarketing phone call for your business. Many people will hesitate before making the call and impose their beliefs on the situation. The little voice will say things like, "I don't like getting telemarketing calls, so the person I am calling won't either." Who knows, the person on the receiving end of the call may need the product or service you are calling them about. What you are doing is transferring your beliefs onto the other person in order to justify not making the call. You are not comfortable making telemarketing calls, so you talk yourself into avoiding it.

We create head trash in many different areas of our life. For a variety of reasons, our inner voice will try to get in the way of our success. Our inner voice will come up with mental images and thoughts to keep us where we are. It may cause you to put yourself down to keep you from making changes. Do you find yourself saying things like, "I can't learn this stuff," or "I'll just make a fool of myself," or "My boss doesn't like me?"

You will find negative thinking occurs in your personal life as well as your business life. We are not immune from it whether you own your own business or work for someone else. Whenever head trash creeps into your thinking you must not allow it to keep you focused on the negatives. Instead, use active positive thinking to change your mental state.

Maintaining your thoughts on the positive outcomes you expect is critical to keeping you moving forward. You are what you think about, and you do what you think about. If you think about the negative outcomes, then you will avoid taking the actions needed. Focus on the positive outcome the action will create for you, like increasing your income or achieving one of your success goals, and you will take positive action.

Using Positive Thoughts to Achieve Success

"Watch your thoughts, they become words, your words become actions, your actions become habits, your habits become character and your character becomes destiny."
— **Frank Outlaw**

Changing your inner voice from negative thinking to positive thinking is a big step in getting the success you want. In the book, *The Secret*, by Rhonda Byrne, the teachers of *The Secret* tell how to use the Law of Attraction to achieve what you want from life. The teachers talk about using the power of thought to attract to you the things you want in life.

Our thoughts and beliefs are real and affect how we perceive our self and our life. Negative thoughts lead to negative feelings. It is a physical impossibility for a negative mind to generate positive thoughts. The habit of negative thinking generates more negative thoughts. It then becomes very difficult to take positive steps toward achieving the success you want. If you are thinking that life is unfair or that life is too hard, then it will be hard for you to make the changes you need. Your inner voice is likely to tell you it doesn't make any difference if you make the change because it probably won't matter anyway.

On the other hand, if you maintain positive thinking and believe life is what you make it, then it will be much easier. Your inner voice will tell you how excited you are to make the changes because it will get you what you want.

Life will give you what you expect it to give you. If you expect bad things, you will get them. If you expect good things, that is what you will get.

You will get good things because you are telling yourself the actions you are taking are going to make a difference. Just thinking about what you want won't create it for you. It is imperative for you to BELIEVE that success is inevitable and to allow your mind to see you achieving your success. You have to believe this to be absolutely true without any hesitation. Your actions will then be the right ones and you will attack them with a passion. Your attention will be focused on the positive things you need to do, not the negative ones. Negative thinking will cause you to second-guess the actions you are taking. If you believe you are not going to succeed or the actions are not going to work, then you will surely fail. You will get more of what you focus on.

Let me give you an example. Try this exercise. Take a minute and look around the room you are sitting in. Take about 20 seconds and find all the green items in the room. Don't write them down; just hold them in your mind. Stop and do this before reading any more or you won't get the point.

Ok, now close your eyes and name all the blue things in the room you can remember. Do you see how your mind filters out what you are not looking for and thinking about? Because you were focused looking for green items (substitute the negative things in your life) you missed the blue things (substitute the positive things). This is why staying focused on what you do want is so important. When you focus on the negative thoughts, those thoughts are what you will see – all the negative things. The converse to that is, if you focus on the positive thoughts you will see the positive things and shut out the negative ones.

Another great example of how this works in your life is from an experiment conducted by psychology graduate students for use in training fighter pilots. In an article in *Best Life*, Guy Martin tells about a tool used in training pilots to stay aware of everything happening while they are flying. The students created a four-minute video showing eight students dribbling and passing basketballs. There were two teams: one dressed in black, one in white, with four students on each team. The students in white pass only to students in white and the students in black only to those in black. All eight students weave among themselves and there is no backboard and no shots taken, just the passing and dribbling. The fighter pilot who is training is asked to watch the video and count how many passes the team in white make to each other. They are to tell the instructor how many passes they make in the air and how many bounce passes they make.

After the video ends, the instructor asks the pilot how many of each he counted. The pilot relates a number to the instructor. The instructor then asks the pilot if he saw the man in the gorilla suit. The stunned pilot says, "What guy in a gorilla suit?" When the instructor replays the video, a man in a gorilla suit walks out and stands in the middle of the students. He stops and then beats his chest for a few seconds before walking off. To the amazement of the pilot, he never saw the gorilla because he was totally focused on counting passes.

How many gorillas do you have in your life that are standing in the middle of your vision of success and you are not noticing? Are you so focused on your day-to-day existence that you don't notice the great opportunities presenting themselves? Negative thinking will keep you focused on the wrong things. It will tend to give you tunnel vision and make it hard to see what is going to make it better. The law of attraction tells us that we will attract what we think about. Use positive thought to creative positive energy and action in your life. This positive energy will lead to taking action on your goals that get you closer every day to the life you want. The momentum will grow with each positive outcome you achieve.

Avoid Negative People and Situations

"I just don't deal with the negativity. I can't get involved in that side of it. I don't understand it, and you can't let it take away from your life and what you are trying to do."
— **Rick Pitino**

Avoiding negative people and situations can be very hard to do some times, but is necessary. You can work hard to keep your own thoughts positive and focused on the successful outcomes you want. But, if you spend a lot of time with other people that are always looking for the negatives and complaining, they will bring you down. These people tend to be pessimists who see life through their own self-limiting beliefs and low self-esteem. They don't see the good side of things. For them the glass is always half empty instead of half full. Avoid these people and don't let them influence your thoughts or behavior.

Negativity breeds more negativity. What you give out in life is what you get back. Give out negative energy and you will get it back. Who are you having lunch with at work? Who is in your inner circle of friends? When you attend business functions, do you stand in a group with the same people and complain about things or surround yourself with high-energy positive people?

If you are a business owner, what is the culture in your company? Have you created a culture that breeds negativity or one that encourages positive behaviors? Have you ever been in a business where the employees were doing nothing but complaining to each other? They may be complaining about the boss or the hours or even the customers.

Recently, I was in a business to drop off some materials the owner had requested. When I first arrived, I had to wait a few minutes for the owner to finish a phone call. I sat in the waiting area but had a clear view of the office staff. The office staff proceeded to talk about their customers that had arranged for service that day. Their comments were unprofessional and negative. The owner walked out of her office and joined them in complaining about a certain client and telling the staff she hoped the customer canceled her service for the day because it was going to be a hassle. I was amazed at the negative culture they had created.

There is no way that business was going to provide great customer service because they simply were not sincere. Their negative attitude was going to come through as they dealt with clients. This business was struggling with growth. The owner told me she was having challenges with her office staff not working well together and mishandling customer requests. Their negative thinking was creating an environment where they expected problems from their customers so that is what they got.

If you own a business or plan to own one someday, it is your responsibility to set the culture of your company. You are accountable for building a business with a culture of positive thinking. Believe that you will succeed, that your team is going to make a positive difference in your company and that your customers are a blessing to you. There is no other choice if you want a business you can be proud to own.

Surround yourself with positive people. Look for people who will lift you up by giving you the attitude of success. Remove negative thinking people from your life.

It may be impossible to remove completely every person who is negative from your life. You can, however, limit their influence on you. If you have a family member, boss or long time friend who fits into the negative thinker category, limit your time with them. When they start their negative comments, look for the good in them and focus on it. Keep your attitude positive and they will either get the message or leave. Otherwise, you will find yourself going down that slippery slope of negativism. You will find that, if you consistently do this, you will start to attract other successful and positive people to you. There is truth in the statement that successful people are attracted to other successful people. Be a positive thinker and you will attract other positive thinkers to your circle of influence.

Develop Self-Confidence

"Your chances of success in any undertaking can always be measured by your belief in yourself."
— **Robert Collier**

Self-confidence is necessary if you are to overcome the negative thoughts holding you back. These negative thoughts are self-limiting beliefs that can be overcome by having the confidence to go after what you want. Changing your self-talk is one of the steps to developing more self-confidence.

Many times when we lack self-confidence, it is due to worrying about what others think about us. We worry what they will think about what we say, how we dress, how we deal with situations or any number of things.

We also worry about disappointing people. We are afraid that if we take action, others may be offended by it or be disappointed we are doing things without them. We also often fear making a mistake. We wonder what others will think if we start out on this journey toward success and make some mistakes along the way. Will they think less of me? Will they laugh at me or talk about me to other people? These are things that get in our way and hold us back.

Self-confidence can grow and blossom if you take the steps to learn how to do it. You can actually begin to feel like a different person inside by gaining the confidence to stand tall and be proud of what you are doing. Here are some things to help you develop more self-confidence:

Learn what a self-confident person is like: A self-confident person is not a cocky, know-it-all person who doesn't care what other people think. They have doubts and they make mistakes the same as everyone else. The difference is, they are willing to acknowledge their shortcomings but don't dwell on them. They maintain a sense of humor and perspective and spend their time focusing on what they have learned from the experience and what is going right. They take things in stride and don't dwell on the negatives.

Spend time with positive people: They understand that people influence our lives, both positively and negatively. By spending time with successful, confident people, you are able to observe their behavior, their way of handling difficult situations and how they relate to people. Learn from these observations and apply them to your own life.

Accept responsibility: Self-confident people accept responsibility for their own happiness and success. They don't wait for others to do this for them. By understanding that you are not a product of your genetic code, but by the choices you make, you are able to take responsibility and will learn self-confidence. Even if something bad happens, they are willing to look at it as a challenge and take responsibility to deal with it.

Don't compare yourself against others: By comparing yourself to others, you undermine your belief of your own value. Usually when you do this, you conclude that you aren't "good enough." Self-confident people appreciate themselves for who they are and for their strengths or accomplishments. They are also willing to acknowledge, without embarrassment, their weaknesses. Be proud of who you are and what you are working to accomplish without worrying about what others are doing.

Don't fear rejection: As you pursue your journey to success, you will encounter rejection. All of us have experienced – and will continue to experience – rejection. Self-confident people don't take rejection personally. Receiving constructive criticism can be very positive for your development. However, sometimes it can be perceived as a form of rejection if you do not have a high level of self-confidence. Remind yourself that you are an achiever and are on a path toward something very special for your life. Don't be afraid to take risks and accept rejection as a learning opportunity to develop strong self-confidence.

Self-confidence is not obstinacy: If a self-confident person has a thought or belief that differs from another person, they will try to look at it from the other person's point of view. They will try to understand it and see why it makes sense to them. They will not try to impose their belief on the other person but keep their own sense of self groundedness. Their own ideas do not fluctuate based on what others deem to be important.

Use "I Am" statements daily: Create a list of statements using the words "I Am" to train your mind to know and accept the good things that you are. Create statements such as, "I am a successful business owner," or "I am a great salesperson" or "I am a good person and am happy with whom I am." Write a list of 15 to 20 of these statements and read them to yourself every day. Believe what you write, read it to yourself and you will stay focused on the positive and create self-confidence.

Let the world know who you are: A self-confident person will know they have a right to go for their dreams. They understand the path may not be easy and there will be mistakes and failures along the way. Still, they are not afraid to let people know what they want and that they are willing to work for it.

Your Subconscious Mind

"It is a psychological law that whatever we wish to accomplish we must impress on the subjective or subconscious mind."
– Orison Swett Marden

Everyone has two different minds, the conscious and the subconscious. The conscious mind is our thinking, which uses logic, deduction, reason and sound judgment to make its decisions. The choices we make in life are made by the conscious mind. The subconscious mind lies outside your conscious mind and has access to data, information and ideas outside your own experience. Your subconscious mind works 24 hours a day. It is the source of all problem solving and goal achievement. It is a magical part of your mind.

Our subconscious mind is unable to distinguish between positive and negative thoughts. Through your subconscious mind, you can come to believe whatever you tell yourself. Tell yourself a positive thought enough times and long enough and your subconscious mind will create it as real. The same is true if you tell yourself negative things enough times. Your subconscious mind strives to attract what you think about and believe based on your most frequent and prominent thoughts.

It is impossible for a negative mind to attract positive things. Your most consistent thoughts will lead your mind to look for and attract what you tell it to seek. The more you train it to look for negative things, the harder it is for it to see the positive. Achieving unlimited success requires you to train your mind to see the positive. Look for those things that will attract success to you by taking action on your plans and goals.

Condition your mind to think positive thoughts, and learn to recognize when head trash starts to creep into your thinking. When you start to hear the little voice in your head create self-doubt, change your thinking. If you begin to feel a lack of self-confidence, stop and adjust your attitude about your abilities and beliefs. If you start to hear yourself saying why you can't do something you want, stop.

Turn your negative language into positive language and tell yourself why you can do it. You condition your mind by being aware of your conscious thoughts and not tolerating negative thoughts. Don't allow them to stay in your mind, or when they do creep in, change them immediately. Over time you will find that you will have fewer negative thoughts the more you focus on removing them and replacing them with positive ones.

Summary

While it is impossible to remove all negative thinking from your life, you can limit its impact. You can control it and not allow the negative thoughts that do sneak in to take over and hold you back. You choose how you react to these thoughts. Each time you get a negative thought, replace it with a positive one. Remove any negative thoughts one at a time until you are focused only on the positive outcomes you want.

Creating a mission for your life, developing your vision of success and setting goals are all key elements of this process of developing self-confidence. You will find that by developing a firm resolve to reach your goals, you will become more self-confident. Success breeds more success and builds your confidence. It is that feeling of confidence that can banish negativity and procrastination and get you moving in the right direction.

Self-confidence is not something you learn overnight. However, it is virtually impossible for a self-confident person to become stuck in a negative thought pattern for very long. Developing your self-confidence will help to keep your mind focused on positive thoughts and reduce the amount of head trash. When you believe in what you are doing and are committed to your actions, confidence will be natural.

Positive thoughts will lead to success. It is a critical element to removing your self-limiting beliefs and living the life of your dreams. In order to get out of your own way and create the life you want, you need to believe absolutely that you will succeed. Believing in yourself and using positive thought to give you the energy, focus and drive to make the changes in your life is critical. Whatever it is in life you want, you must begin today to be a positive thinker to achieve the success you have defined for yourself. Once you do this, you will be able to achieve unlimited success.

CHAPTER 13

Choosing to Live the Life of Your Dreams

"Take the first step in faith. You don't have to see the whole staircase, just take the first step."
— **Martin Luther King Jr.**

You have now taken a big step toward achieving the unlimited success of your dreams. You have identified what success means to you and established the vision of what it will look like. The goals you have set will take you along a path to where you want to go in life. Now you get to choose how to apply all that you have learned to get what you want. You now understand what self-limiting beliefs are and how to remove them as roadblocks. The power of choice is a wonderful gift; use this gift to get what you want from life. It is your choice to follow along the path of success or stay where you are and simply dream about what might be. What path will you choose to follow?

A lot of material has been written on how to achieve your dreams effortlessly. Advertising messages tell us how to achieve results without working hard or putting forth any real effort. Understanding that a key ingredient to success is taking action will help you avoid this trap. Regardless of what other messages tell you, there is no easy way out. Action and perseverance are required, and your goals will tell you just how much action it will take. For those individuals that create a plan for their life and take action, success is their reward. You must be willing to put forth the extra effort that gets you to the next level. Many times it is that little bit of extra effort that pushes you to the next level of success.

There is a great book titled *212° the Extra Degree* by Sam Parker and Mac Anderson. In the book, they tell how at 211° water is hot, but at 212° water boils. The extra degree changes the water from a liquid to steam creating a completely different kind of energy. That one extra degree creates enough force to power a machine. If you want to make meaningful change, you need to be willing to put forth that extra degree of effort to transform your life. There is great power in being willing to take a step every day and not give up. Sticking to your goals and pushing through challenges with an extra degree of effort will create a power that cannot be stopped. Choose to put forth that effort starting today.

Largely the books you read, the people you meet and the actions you take, will determine the quality of life that you live. There are hundreds of great books, CDs, DVDs and on-line e-zines available to help you. Look for the ones that can help you stay focused and learn what you need. Constantly make a point of meeting new people that you can learn from. Be willing to put yourself out there by not being afraid of introducing yourself to people in your area of interest. You will be surprised how much people will help if you just ask and are sincere in your interest. The actions you take will determine much of what you achieve.

Getting Out of Your Own Way

"Life is just a mirror, and what you see out there, you must first see inside of you."
– Wally "Famous" Amos

Much of this book has been focused on helping you determine what you need to do to get out of your own way. Our self-limiting beliefs are so much of what holds us back. You must choose to accept the idea that you are being held back by negative beliefs or beliefs that your abilities are limited. Another key factor of getting out of your own way is to understand that you must unlearn some things you have believed all your life.

From the earliest stage of our life, we have been taught ideas that limit our beliefs. Some of these are beliefs about money and success. Many people believe that the rich became rich by being greedy or taking advantage of others. We are taught that pursuing wealth or our own dreams makes us self-centered, and that we should always be thinking about others rather than about what we want. We are also taught that in order to be a good person, we must be willing to sacrifice our dreams. We are taught to seek security and avoid risk. Many people believe you should work at the same job for 50 or more years and retire with whatever you have been able to save. They feel the most you should hope for is a steady paycheck, a roof over your head and food on the table. Wanting anything more than this is selfish or risky.

If you harbor any of these ideas, you must unlearn them and change your thinking. Since you have read this book, it is safe to say you are looking for something more in life. You are to be congratulated for this.

Life is meant to be lived to the fullest, and there is nothing wrong with having dreams and pursuing them regardless of what you may have been taught in the past.

Your success mind-set will determine what you choose to do with your life. Create new beliefs that money and success are good.

Wealth is something to be pursued and admired. The truth is most people who have achieved wealth are good hard working people just like you.

There are 8.7 million millionaires in the world. The number of new millionaires is increasing every year. There is no reason why you cannot be one of the new millionaires. In the book *The Millionaire Next Door*, by Thomas J. Stanley and William D. Danko, they give the following statistics: Eighty percent of America's millionaires are first-generation wealthy. This is contrary to those who would have you believe that wealth is usually inherited. Twenty percent of millionaires created wealth through retirement planning and 50 percent of millionaires own a business. It is very telling that 50 percent of America's millionaires own a business. Combine the 50 percent who are business owners with the 20 percent who built wealth through retirement planning and this accounts for 70 percent of all millionaires. Based on these statistics, it is easy to see the road to wealth is more often not through receiving a steady paycheck. The people who pursue their dreams are more likely to achieve wealth than those that don't. If one of your success measures is to attain wealth, then you may need to unlearn your old beliefs about money.

Look inside yourself and find what is holding you back. Seek out books or programs that can help you adjust your thinking. Life is a mirror and it reflects back what you believe. Unlearn the negative beliefs you may have and replace them with mental images of success.

Talk to your mentor about these beliefs, and ask for help to identify ways to change your thinking. Have them hold you accountable if you start to fall into the old thought pattern. The sooner you change how you think about wealth and success, the faster you will be able to make progress toward your goals and dreams.

Choose to Win

*"It is hard to fail, but it is worse never
to have tried to succeed."*
– **Theodore Roosevelt**

Choosing to live the life of your dreams requires you to stay focused on your end result and to never lose faith in yourself or your plan.

Did you know that in 1911, the L.L. Bean Company almost went broke? It was their first year in business, and the company sold its first 100 pair of hunting shoes that all had flaws that caused them to fall apart. Company founder, Leon Leonwood Bean, took out a loan to replace them, and that launched the company's now famous money-back guarantee. Bean believed in his dream and refused to give up when he hit adversity. He had faith in himself and his vision that took him to great success. Bean could have accepted the failure and moved on with the disappointment of his failure. Choose to overcome the small failures on your journey to reach your goals just as Bean did. A little more effort and what seems hopeless may turn into a glorious success.

**Before you can win at life, you need to have a
reason greater than your current reality.**

If you ask most people if they want to be rich or successful, they will say yes. But, then reality sets in and the road seems too long and hard. There are too many hills to climb and it is easier to continue doing what they are doing today. Your reason for working toward success must be your own. You must be doing it for yourself and those you love. If you are doing it for any other reason, your chance of success is limited. We started this book by defining your definition of success. Keep going back to that purpose on a regular basis, and make sure the win you are aiming for ties into your definition of success.

Realistically, with every step you take in the process, you have the power to choose your future. You can choose to live the life you want or to live the life you have today. You may be very happy with your life today and that is wonderful. Still, you may want more, and your vision for your life will lead you to a different place. Those who choose not to move toward their dreams by taking action every day are choosing to stay where they are. Understand what drives you, and use it to fuel your passion to win. Don't let anyone or anything get in the way of what is rightfully yours.

Don't Expect Overnight Miracles

"He that can have patience can have what he will."
— **Benjamin Franklin**

The journey to success is not an overnight one. Keep in mind that it took many years to get where you are today. It will take some time to make the changes you want and reach your dreams. It is important that you start out on your journey knowing that. Unless you have realistic expectations of what it's going to take, you will become frustrated and be tempted to give up on your dream.

This is a very common situation in the coaching arena. People come into a coaching program expecting overnight results, and after a few months, they start to get frustrated. We actually disclose to them at the beginning of a program that this is going to occur. It is a natural reaction. A business owner who has operated her business for more than 20 years may have been struggling for the last several years to build the business she wanted. The profits aren't as high as she expected and she may be working way too many hours. Her personal life is suffering due to the stress level. Yet, this owner will come into a coaching program looking to improve her situation and expect it to change immediately. It took 20 years to get where they are today, so it is going to take a few years to change it. That is just a fact. It will take time to gain the skills and knowledge you may need. The process of changing old habits and thinking differently takes time. Don't set yourself up for disappointment by giving yourself unrealistic time frames to achieve your goals.

Patience is a virtue that can be very hard to deal with. As a society, we are conditioned for instant gratification. Our society moves faster and faster every day. Technology has created a belief that we should have instant access to everything we want. Unfortunately, life does not work the same way when we are attempting to create a different reality. Instead, you must be willing to stick with your plan as long as it takes.

Success is a learnable skill that is created over time with attention and dedication to your dreams. You must nurture your dreams and tend to them daily through your actions and thoughts.

Anyone who has achieved a high level of success did it through deliberate focus on his or her end goal. It takes years for a professional golfer, concert pianist or a world-class chef to learn the skills that took them to the top of their profession. The same is true about becoming a successful entrepreneur or achieving success in your career. To become the top salesperson in your company or achieve a senior executive level position will take time and effort. Keep your focus on the end result you are looking for and measure your progress along the way. This is how you will be choosing success as your life's mission.

Choose to Work on You

> *"Become addicted to constant and never ending self improvement."*
> – Anthony J. D'Angelo

The fastest way to success is to continuously work harder on yourself than you do on your career or your business. Doing so will lead to the results you are seeking. Many times we tend to think more about the task at hand and what needs to be done today. Instead, spend time each day deciding what you need to do to improve yourself. Your skills, beliefs, confidence and results will increase dramatically when you do.

Think about it this way. When an oak tree first starts to grow, it is seeded by an acorn. Growing from the acorn in the wild, the oak sapling will develop a single hair-thin tap root. This tap root will extend deep into the ground looking for water and may grow as deep as three feet when the sapling is only a foot tall. When the sapling is grown in a commercial nursery, the tap root tends to grow in a coil at the bottom of the pot. Many times the tap root will be broken off when the tree is transplanted. A good gardener will create a deep hole in the ground with a long metal rod. He will then weight down the tender root and feed it down into the hole. This little bit of extra effort will ensure its life and allow it to develop much faster and stronger. Invest this same care into your own development. Take the time to develop the strong roots you need to achieve success. When you plant a garden, you feed the roots in order to grow strong healthy flowers or vegetables. You must feed your spirit and mind in the same way. Doing so will create the results you seek.

The Japanese term Kaizen means "Constant and never ending improvement." It promotes continual, incremental improvements in all areas of business and life. The Japanese used this philosophy to create automobiles that have shaken the U.S. auto industry. Kaizen is actually a way of life philosophy. It assumes that every aspect of our life deserves to be constantly improved. The same philosophy is important for you to use on your journey toward success. This journey does not require you to make immediate major improvements every day. The important thing is to work on constantly improving your skills, beliefs and knowledge. One step at a time will still get you there.

The first step to improving your beliefs is to identify what beliefs you have and then decide whether they are helping or hurting your progress. You listed the beliefs holding you back earlier in this book, but understand that this is a never ending process. You will need to take time occasionally to stop and review your current belief system. Time and circumstances will change your beliefs. By taking positive steps every day, you will begin to see many of your old beliefs change for the better. Still, there will be some new beliefs that creep into your thinking as you move forward. Some of them will be positive and some will not. To make the constant and never ending self-improvement essential to success, you need to remain aware of your beliefs.

If you want to change the visible components of your life, you need to first change the invisible.

If you want to improve your wealth, business, relationships, health and possessions, then first change you. Changing your beliefs and working on your skills and knowledge are important steps if you are choosing to follow a path to success.

Putting It All Together

By now you should have a very good idea of what you want from life and what you need to do to get it. You have done a lot of self-discovery about what is holding you back. You are ready to start taking the steps necessary to live your dreams. You may be feeling some extra motivation and are excited about getting started. Before you do, go back and review the action plan you have developed so far.

As you progressed through this book, you probably had some additional thoughts and ideas you wanted to add to your plan. Review your definition of success one more time and make any necessary adjustments. Then review your vision statements and make any adjustments in order to make these vision statements as clear and focused as possible. Once you are completely satisfied with these, type them up, print them out and put them someplace they can be reviewed regularly.

Review the goals and the 90-day planner you wrote in chapter 4 and refine them. This will become your launch point for the action you will start taking toward your success plan. Finalize your first action steps on the 90-day plan. Be careful not to overestimate what you can realistically accomplish in the next 90 days. It is a mistake to expect to do too much and potentially set yourself up for disappointment. In order to build momentum, give yourself a few important goals to focus on first. Make these meaningful but achievable. Once you start to see success against these first few goals, it will give you the enthusiasm to keep going.

Be sure that – as you look at what objectives you are setting for your 90-day plan – you also consider the self-limiting beliefs you identified. You should be working on changing the most important of these beliefs right from the beginning. Do not allow yourself to ignore these self-limiting beliefs. You must consciously work on them from the beginning. They will not just go away or change themselves. It has taken many years for you to develop them, and it will take some effort and time to change them.

It would be advisable to include choosing a mentor to help you as one of your first goals. Having someone to hold you accountable and guide you will be very powerful. Do not underestimate the importance of this. It may still take some effort to set up the relationship to work for you, so setting it as a goal is advisable. If you don't have someone in mind, then set that as your goal. Identify potential mentors and work through the process to find the right one for you.

Once you have taken these steps, it is time to get started.

Summary

"So many fail because they don't get started – they don't go. They don't overcome inertia. They don't begin."
— W. Clement Stone

You have made a lot of decisions during the course of this book. By completing the worksheets provided, you now have the information you need to get started on building the life you want. A final thought to leave you with: Start now! Don't start living tomorrow, tomorrow never arrives. Start working on your dreams and ambitions today. In order to achieve the success you want, you need to get started.

It is so easy to get excited about making changes and setting a plan for your business or your life. Many times though, we tell ourselves we will start on it in a little while. Maybe there is something you are doing now and decide to wait until you have finished it first. The reality is, most of the time you will lose some of your excitement and momentum and will never get started. When you do finally start, you may have less enthusiasm. Don't take that risk.

Success should be what you decide it is. Just thinking about success as you defined it should get you excited and make you happy.

> **Your heart must lead you through this journey; for surely a passionate life is a life worth living.**

The life you are going to build should be one that you can pursue passionately. Pulitzer prize columnist and author Anna Quindlen is quoted as saying,

> *"If your success is not on your own terms, if it looks good to the world but does not feel good in your heart, it is not success at all."*

Success must be on your own terms and look and feel good to you. It must be something you can pursue with your heart as well as your head. Life is meant to be lived to the fullest. Don't let another minute go by without knowing what you want, and be willing to commit to it 100 percent everyday. The only thing that keeps you from having all that you want is you! Learn how to get out of your own way and do not let fear or doubt or any other self-limiting belief keep you from getting all you desire. Time is a very precious asset and you must use it wisely. However, time can also be a liability if you don't use it right. It is a limited commodity, and you must learn how to prioritize your time toward the pursuit of your dreams.

Start your journey today. Lead your life in the pursuit of success and happiness will follow. Believe in yourself and your dreams and don't let anyone deter you from your mission. The life you want is waiting for you. You deserve to have what you want, and all you need to do is decide to go and get it!

I challenge you to never give up pursuing success. Fight for it every day against all that life will try to throw at you. Look for inspiration whenever you need it. It is all around you. There are countless stories throughout the ages of people who achieved amazing levels of success against the greatest of odds. Now it is time for you to write your story of success.

Good luck and God bless!

"Within you right now is the power to do things you never dreamed possible. This power becomes available to you just as soon as you change your beliefs."

— **Maxwell Maltz**

Recommended Reading

212° the Extra Degree – Sam Parker & Mac Anderson
Billionaire in Training – Bradley J. Sugars
Building the Happiness-Centered Business – Dr. Paddi Lund
Buzzoodle Buzz Marketing – Ron McDaniel
Creating Your Own Destiny – Patrick Snow
Customer Satisfaction is WORTHLESS; Customer Loyalty is Priceless – Jeffrey Gitomer
Developing the Leader Within – John C. Maxwell
Developing the Leaders Around You – John C. Maxwell
Eat That Frog – Brian Tracy
Fish – Stephen C. Lundin, Ph.D., Harry Paul and John Christensen
Getting Things Done – David Allen
Good To Great – Jim Collins
How to Read a Financial Report – John A. Tracy
How to Win Friends and Influence People – Dale Carnegie
Jesus CEO – Laurie Beth Jones
Little Red Book of Sales – Jeffrey Gitomer
Oh the Places You'll Go – Dr. Seuss
Rich Dad Poor Dad – Robert T. Kiyosaki
Riches in Niches – Susan Friedman
Selling the Invisible – Harry Beckwith
The 7 Habits of Highly Effective People – Stephen R. Covey
The Business Coach – Bradley J. Sugars
The E-Myth Revisited – Michael E. Gerber
The Five Dysfunctions of a Team – Patrick Lencioni
The Fred Factor – Mark Sanborn
The Strangest Secret – Earl Nightingale
The Leadership Secrets of Colin Powell – Oren Harari
The Secret – Rhonda Byrne
Think & Grow Rich – Napoleon Hill
Who Moved My Cheese – Spencer Johnson, M.D.

About the Author

Dennis Kelley, founder of The D. Kelley Group, is an author, coach, speaker and trainer. Through his business, he provides professional coaching, motivational and keynote speaking services. His popular seminars have helped achievement-minded individuals learn the keys to success in business and life. As a certified business coach, author and speaker, Dennis helps business owners and professionals achieve new levels of success in life and business.

Dennis has over 31 years of business and executive leadership experience and has spent many of these years leading diverse teams in the financial services industry. He has applied his experience in corporate America to coaching business owners and professionals on how to achieve greater success. Through his coaching business, he helps people unleash the potential hidden within and remove the self-limiting beliefs holding them back.

Get more information and free resources at
www.AchievingUnlimitedSuccess.com.

About *The D. Kelley Group*

Now that you have completed this book and defined what you want from life, you may decide you need support to help you reach your goals. Coaching is a powerful way to ensure you stay focused and on track to achieve the success you desire. At The D. Kelley Group, we provide professional coaching, speaking and training services to guide you, teach you and hold you accountable to your action plan.

We offer business coaching to entrepreneurs and professionals interested in achieving new levels of success in their business and life. Our program uses a proven process to improve profitability, reduce the amount of time you spend working in the business and develop a winning team to support your goals. You will begin to think differently about your business or career and your ability to achieve the highest level of success.

We will work with you to teach, train, guide and counsel you. As an accountability partner, we will keep you engaged in the activities required to achieve the success you seek.

Dennis provides keynote speeches to groups or conferences. Visit our Website at www.AchievingUnlimitedSuccess.com and click on the coaching tab to learn more about our coaching or speaking services. One of our coaches will provide you with a free one-hour consultation to assess your suitability for coaching.

E-mail me at Dennis@AchievingUnlimitedSuccess.com and tell me a little about what you would like to achieve, and I will match a coach to your needs and have them contact you to arrange your free consultation.

Taking action is one of the critical steps to *Achieving Unlimited Success* in your life. Start today by requesting your free consultation.